a

INTRODUCTION

Quick Reference Guide for WordPerfect 5.0™ is a handy guide that will save hours searching through technical manuals. Each step is pictured, so a quick glance at the key illustrations will walk you through the procedures. The most commonly used word processing features and WordPerfect's desktop publishing features are included.

An index, referencing all procedures covered in the book, appears on pages 156 - 159.

It is our hope this book will help you enjoy the benefits of WordPerfect 5.0™ with ease.

Zachary O. Auslander
Marivel Salazar

Technical Editor
Zachary O. Auslander

14East 38th Street, New York, NY 10016

WORDPERFECT KEYBOARD

b

C

FUNCTION KEY Illustrations

F1	Cancel/Undelete
Alt + F1	Thesaurus
Shift + F1	Setup
Ctrl + F1	Shell (DOS access)
F2	Forward Search
Alt + F2	Replace
Shift + F2	Reverse Search
Ctrl + F2	Speller
F3	Help
Alt + F3	Reveal Codes
Shift + F3	Switch
Ctrl + F3	Screen Options
F4	Left Indent
Alt + F4	Block On/Off
Shift + F4	Left/Right Indent
Ctrl + F4	Move Menu
F5	List Files
Alt + F5	Mark Text Menu
Shift + F5	Date/Outline
Ctrl + F5	Text In/Out Menu
F6	Bold
Alt + F6	Flush Right
Shift + F6	Center
Ctrl + F6	Tab Align
F7	Exit
Alt + F7	Math/Columns Menu
Shift + F7	Print Menu
Ctrl + F7	Footnote Menu
F8	Underline
Alt + F8	Style
Shift + F8	Format Menu
Ctrl + F8	Font Menu
F9	Merge Code ^R
Alt + F9	Graphics
Shift + F9	Merge Codes
Ctrl + F9	Merge/Sort Menu
F10	Save
Alt + F10	Execute Macro
Shift + F10	Retrieve
Ctrl + F10	Define Macro

For the extended keyboard:

F11	Reveal Codes
F12	Block On/Off

USING DOS TO FORMAT A DISK

For two floppy disk drives

1. Insert DOS Systems Disk into Drive A.
2. Turn the computer on.
3. Type the Date (XX-XX-XX).
4. ENTER.
5. Type the Time (XX:XX).
6. ENTER.
7. At the A> type FORMAT B:
8. ENTER.
9. Insert a NEW disk into Drive B.
10. ENTER to begin the formatting procedure.
11. When the procedure is completed, type Y to format another disk or N to return to the prompt.

For a hard disk drive with floppy disk drive

1. Turn the computer on.
2. Type FORMAT A:

   NOTE: Verify at the C>, and a path has been set to the DOS directory.

3. ENTER.
4. Insert a NEW disk into Drive A.
5. ENTER to begin the formatting procedure.
6. When the procedure is completed, type Y to format another disk or N to return to the prompt.

STARTUP PROCEDURE/LOADING

For two floppy disk drives

1. Insert DOS disk into drive A.

   NOTE: DOS disk must have config.sys file with a minimum of files=20 and buffers=5.

2. Turn computer on.
3. Type DATE (XX-XX-XX).
4. ENTER.
5. Type TIME (XX:XX).
6. ENTER.
7. Insert the WordPerfect 1 disk into drive A.
8. Insert data disk into drive B.
9. Type B:
10. ENTER.
11. Type A:wp.
12. ENTER.
13. When prompted, replace Wordperfect 1 disk with WordPerfect 2 disk.
14. ENTER.

    NOTE: Steps 13-14 are not required for 3.5 disks.

For hard disk drive with floppy disk drive

1. Turn computer on.

   NOTE: Drive c: must have config.sys file with a minimum of files=20 and buffers=5.

2. Insert data disk into drive A.
3. Change to WordPerfect directory (type CD\directory name).
4. Type A:
5. ENTER.
6. Type C:wp.
7. ENTER.

CREATE A DOCUMENT

NOTE: After starting WordPerfect, the cursor will blink in the top left-hand corner of the screen. The status line appears in the bottom right-hand corner of the screen, and displays the document number, page number, line and cursor position. The line and position are measured in inches.

Begin typing the text.

Example: Doc 1 Pg 1 Ln 1" Pos 1"

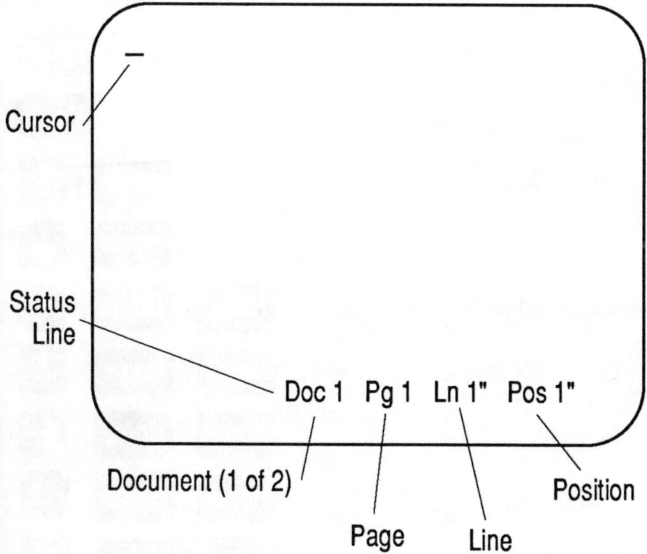

CURSOR MOVEMENTS WITHIN A DOCUMENT

One character left	←
One character right	→
One line Up	↑
One line down	↓
Previous word	Ctrl + ←
Next word	Ctrl + →
Top of previous page	PgUp
Top of next page	PgDn
Top of screen	Home + ↑
End of screen	Home + ↓
Beginning of document	Home, Home, ↑
End of document	Home, Home, ↓
Beginning of Line	Home, Home, ←
End of Line	Home, Home, →
Top of page	Ctrl + Home, ↑
Bottom of Page	Ctrl + Home, ↓

CURSOR MOVEMENTS USING THE GO TO KEY

TO A SPECIFIC CHARACTER

1. Press **Ctrl + Home** (Go To Key)............... Ctrl + Home
2. Type character.. **Option**

TO A SPECIFIC PAGE

1. Press **Ctrl + Home** (Go To Key)............... Ctrl + Home
2. Type page number...**Option**
3. Enter.. ↵

SAVING A DOCUMENT AND CLEARING SCREEN

SAVE AND CONTINUE WORKING ON A NEW DOCUMENT

1. Press **F1O** (Save).. F10
2. Type name of document................................. **Option**

   NOTE: It may be necessary to indicate drive and/or directory when entering document name.
   ***Example:** A:letter*

3. Enter.. ↵

SAVE AND EXIT A NEW DOCUMENT

1. Press **F7**.. F7
2. Enter.. ↵
3. Type name of document................................. **Option**

   NOTE: It may be necessary to indicate drive and/or directory when entering document name.
   ***Example:** A:letter*

4. Enter.. ↵
5. Enter (to continue in WordPerfect)...................... ↵

continued...

Saving a document and clearing screen (continued)

DOCUMENT PREVIOUSLY SAVED

1. Press **F7**.. F7
2. Enter.. ↵
3. Enter (to retain same document name)..................... ↵
4. Select **Y** (to update document with revisions).......... Y
5. Enter (to continue in WordPerfect).......................... ↵

CLEAR SCREEN (WITHOUT SAVING DOCUMENT)

1. Press **F7**.. F7
2. Select **N**.. N
3. Enter.. ↵

RETRIEVE A DOCUMENT

NOTE: If document is on screen see SAVING A DOCUMENT AND CLEARING SCREEN

1. Press **Shift + F10** (Retrieve)...................... Shift + F10

NOTE: It may be necessary to indicate drive and/or directory when entering document name. ***Example:*** *A:letter*

2. Type name of document to be retrieved.................**Option**

3. Enter..

OR

LIST FILES

1. Press **F5**.. F5

NOTE: If necessary specify drive and/or directory to access files. ***Example:*** *A:*

2. Enter..

3. Place cursor on document to be retrieved using cursor movement keys.

4. Select **R** (Retrieve).. R

BLOCK TEXT (HIGHLIGHTING)

(for DELETE, MOVE, REPLACE, UNDERLINE, CENTER, CASE CONVERSION, SORT, SPELL, BOLD, FLUSH RIGHT, PRINT, APPEND, COMMENT, FONT, MARK TEXT, PROTECT, and STYLE)

1. Place cursor on first character of text to be highlighted.
2. Press **Alt + F4** (Block On/Off)........................ **Alt** + **F4**

   NOTE: A flashing "Block on" message appears at the bottom left-hand corner of screen.

3. Highlight text to be defined: **Option**

   One character to the right.. **→**

   One word to the right.................................... **Ctrl** + **→**

   End of line.. **End**

   One line up... **↑**

   One line down.. **↓**

   A sentence.................................... **Punctuation Mark**

   A paragraph.. **↵**

   End of screen.................................... **Home** + **↓**

   End of page.. **PgDn**

   Several pages

   a) Press **Ctrl + Home** (Go To)........... **Ctrl** + **Home**

   b) Type page number....................................... **Option**

   NOTE: This highlights up to the beginning of the selected page number.

   c) Enter... **↵**

   NOTE: Typing a character will highlight up to that character.

4. Refer to appropriate section (from above list) to execute specific function.

EDITING TEXT

INSERTING TEXT

NOTE: WordPerfect defaults to insert mode, if "Typeover" message appears in the bottom left corner press the Insert key again.

1. Place cursor where text is to be inserted.
2. Type text.

TYPEOVER

1. Place cursor where text is to be overwritten.
2. Press **Insert** .... Ins

   NOTE: Typeover" message appears in the bottom left corner.

3. Type text.
4. Press **Insert** .... Ins

continued...

DELETE

Character

1. Place cursor on character to be deleted.
2. Press **Delete**.. Del

Previous character

1. Place cursor immediately after character to be deleted.
2. Press **Backspace**...................................... Backspace

Word

1. Place cursor on word to be deleted.
2. Press **Ctrl + Backspace** .... Ctrl + Backspace

Parts of a word

Press **Home + Backspace** (to delete from left of cursor to beginning of the word) .... Home + Backspace

Press **Home + Delete** (to delete from cursor to next word).. Home + Del

continued...

TO THE END OF THE LINE

1. Place cursor on first character to be deleted.
2. Press **Ctrl + End** .... Ctrl + End

TO THE END OF PAGE

1. Place cursor on first character to be deleted.
2. Press **Ctrl + PgDn**................................ Ctrl + PgDn
3. Select **Y** (to delete remainder of page).................. Y

SEVERAL LINES (ESCAPE KEY)

1. Place cursor on first character of line to be deleted.
2. Press **Escape**.. Esc
3. Type number of lines to be deleted.................... **Option**
4. Press **Ctrl + End**...................................... Ctrl + End

DELETE USING BLOCK HIGHLIGHT

1. Place cursor on first character to be deleted.
2. Press **Alt + F4** (Block On/Off)...................... Alt + F4
3. Highlight text. (See Block Text section.)
4. Press **Delete**.. Del
5. Select **Y** (to delete block)...................................... Y

DELETE CODES

1. Press **Alt + F3** (Reveal Codes).................... Alt + F3
2. Place cursor on code to be deleted.
3. Press **Delete**.. Del
4. Press **Alt + F3** (Exit Reveal Codes).............. Alt + F3

UNDELETE

1. Place cursor where deleted text will be inserted.
2. Press **F1** (Undelete).. F1
3. Select **R** (Restore).. R

   or OR

   a) Press **P** (until desired deletion appears)........ P

   NOTE: The last three deletions can be displayed.

   b) Select **R** (Restore).. R

DOCUMENT SUMMARY

CREATE/EDIT

1. Retrieve document.
2. Press **Shift + F8** (Format menu)................ Shift + F8
3. Select **D** (Document).. D
4. Select **S** (Summary).. S

   NOTE: Document name and creation date are entered by the computer.

5. Select **D** (Descriptive Filename).............................. D
6. Edit text.
7. Enter.. ↵
8. Select **S** (Subject/Account).. S
9. Edit text.
10. Enter.. ↵
11. Select **A** (Author).. A
12. Edit text.
13. Enter.. ↵
14. Select **T** (Typist).. T
15. Edit text.
16. Enter.. ↵
17. Select **C** (Comment)... C
18. Edit text.
19. Press **F7**... F7
20. Press **F7** (return to document)................................ F7

PRINTING

NOTE: Printer must be selected during installation for printing to be successful.

A STORED DOCUMENT

1. Press **Shift + F7** (Print menu).................... Shift + F7
2. Select **D** (Document on disk)................................ D
3. Type name of document....................................... **Option**

   NOTE: It may be necessary to indicate drive and/or directory when entering document name.
   Example: *A:letter*

4. Enter.. ↵
5. Enter (to print entire document)............................ ↵

   or OR

   a) Type page(s) with commas and dashes.

Examples:	
- 3	Page 1-3
2, 5	Page 2 and 5
4-9	Pages 4-9
6-	Pages 6 to last page
-3, 8-10, 13	Pages 1-3, 8-10, 13

   b) Enter.. ↵

   NOTE: Type "y" if prompted.

6. Press **F7** (Exit Printer menu)................................ F7

DOCUMENT ON SCREEN

1. Press **Shift + F7** (Print menu).................... Shift + F7
2. Select **F** (Full Document).. F

   or OR

   Select **P** (Page)... P

continued...

VIEW DOCUMENT ON SCREEN

NOTE: A graphics card or color monitor is necessary for the view feature to function.

1. Press **Shift + F7** (Print menu)...................... Shift + F7

2. Select **V** (View Document).. V

3. Select from one of the following view options: **Option**

   a) Select **1** (100%).. 1

   b) Select **2** (200%).. 2

   c) Select **3** (Full Page)... 3

   d) Select **4** (Facing Pages)..................................... 4

NOTE: Facing Pages displays the facing even and odd page.

4. Press **F7** (return to document)..................................... F7

continued...

PRINT BLOCK

1. Place cursor on first character to be printed.
2. Press **Alt + F4** (Block On/Off)...................... **Alt** + **F4**
3. Highlight text. (See Block Text section.)
4. Press **Shift + F7** (Print menu)................... **Shift** + **F7**
5. Select **Y** (to print block).. **Y**

LIST FILES

1. Press **F5** (List Files).. **F5**

   NOTE: If necessary, change drive/directory to access files

2. Enter.. ↵
3. Press arrow keys to highlight document to be printed.
4. Select **P** (print)... **P**
5. Enter (to print entire document)................................ ↵

   or OR

   a) Type page(s) with commas and dashes.

Examples:	
-3	Page 1-3
2,5	Page 2 and 5
4-9	Pages 4-9
6-	Pages 6 to last page
-3, 8-10, 13	Pages 1-3, 8-10, 13

   b) Enter.. ↵

   NOTE: Type "y" if prompted.

6. Press **F7** (to exit List Files)... **F7**

continued...

CANCELLING A PRINT REQUEST

Interrupt and resume printing

1. Press **Shift + F7** (Print menu).................. Shift + F7
2. Select **C** (Control Printer).. C
3. Select **S** (Stop).. S

   NOTE: Type "y" to confirm if requested.

4. Make any necessary changes to printer.
5. Select **G** (Go - Start Printer).................................... G

   NOTE: Press Enter if necessary.

Cancel print job before printing begins

1. Press **Shift + F7** (Print menu).................. Shift + F7
2. Select **C** (Control Printer) C
3. Select **C** (Cancel Job[s])... C
4. Type job number to cancel................................. **Option**
5. Enter (to cancel print job)... ↵

   NOTE: Type "y" or "c" to confirm if requested.

6. Press **F7** (Exit)... F7

   NOTE: Cancelling a print request may not work if the printer has a large buffer. See printer manual for details.

continued...

View list of print jobs

1. Press **Shift + F7** (Print menu).................... Shift + F7
2. Select **C** (Control Printer).. C
3. If four or more jobs:
   A) Select **D** (Display Jobs) .... D
   B) Press **F7** F7
4. Press **F7** (Exit).. F7

TYPE THROUGH

To use printer like a typewriter.

NOTE: Printer must support this feature.

CHARACTER TYPE THROUGH

1. Press **Shift + F7** (Print menu).................... Shift + F7
2. Select **Y** (Type Through)... Y
3. Select **C** (Character).. C
4. Press Space Bar until cursor is at desired location.
5. Type character..**Option**
6. Repeat steps 4 and 5 for all characters to be printed.
7. Press **F7** F7
8. Press **F7** (Exit Print menu).. F7

LINE TYPE THROUGH

1. Press **Shift + F7** (Print menu).................... Shift + F7
2. Select **Y** (Type Through)... Y
3. Select **L** (Line).. L
4. Type text.

   NOTE: Line may be edited.

5. Enter (to print line)... ↵
6. Repeat steps 4 and 5 for each line to be printed.
7. Press **F7** F7
8. Press **F7** (Exit Print menu).. F7

DOCUMENT ASSEMBLY

BOILERPLATE TEXT

1. Clear Screen (see Clear Screen section).
2. Type text for Boilerplate.
3. Press **F7**.. F7
4. Enter (Save document).. ↵
5. Type name of Boilerplate document....................Option
6. Enter.. ↵
7. Enter (Exit to new document screen)..................... ↵

COMBINING DOCUMENTS

1. Press **Shift + F10** (Retrieve).................. Shift + F10
2. Type name of document that will be combined with Boilerplate document....................Option
3. Enter.. ↵
4. Place cursor where Boilerplate will be inserted.
5. Press **Shift + F10** (Retrieve).................. Shift + F10
6. Type name of Boilerplate document.................... Option
7. Enter.. ↵
8. Repeat steps 4-7 for each Boilerplate to be placed.

MARGINS

SETTING LEFT AND RIGHT MARGINS

1. Place cursor at designated location for margin change.

   NOTE: Text after this point will be affected by the margin change.

2. Press **Shift + F8** (Format menu)............... Shift + F8
3. Select **L** (Line)............... L
4. Select **M** (Margin)............... M

   NOTE: Current margins are displayed.

5. Type left margin............... **Option**
6. Enter............... ↵
7. Type right margin............... **Option**
8. Enter............... ↵
9. Press **F7** (return to document)............... F7

SETTING TOP AND BOTTOM MARGIN

1. Place cursor at top of page.
2. Press **Shift + F8** (Format menu)............... Shift + F8
3. Select **P** (Page)............... P
4. Select **M** (Margin)............... M
5. Type top margin............... **Option**
6. Enter............... ↵
7. Type bottom margin............... **Option**
8. Enter............... ↵
9. Press **F7** (return to document)............... F7

MARGIN RELEASE

NOTE: The margin release moves the cursor to the previous tab setting.

1. Place cursor at the beginning of line where margin will be released.
2. Press **Shift + Tab** (Margin Release).......... Shift + Tab

TAB SET

NORMAL STYLE (LEFT-JUSTIFIED)

1. Place cursor at designated location in document for tab change.

   NOTE: Text after this point will be affected by the tab change.

2. Press **Shift + F8** (Format menu).................. Shift + F8
3. Select **L** (Line)... L
4. Select **T** (Tabs).. T
5. Press **Home, Home, Left Arrow**.. Home, Home, ←
6. Press **Ctrl + End** (to clear all tabs)............... Ctrl + End
7. Mark tab settings:

   a) Place cursor at designated location for tab setting.

   b) Type **L**.. L

   or OR

   a) Type position of tab..**Option**

   b) Enter.. ↵

   NOTE: A tab can be deleted by moving cursor under (L) and pressing the delete key.

8. Repeat step 7 for all tabs.
9. Press **F7** F7
10. Press **F7** (return to document)................................ F7

continued...

SPECIAL TAB STYLES

1. Place cursor at designated location in document for tab change.

   NOTE: Text after this point will be affected by the tab change.

2. Press **Shift + F8** (Format menu)................. Shift + F8
3. Select **L** (Line).. L
4. Select **T** (Tabs).. T
5. Press **Home, Home, Left Arrow**.. Home , Home , ←
6. Press **Ctrl + End** (to clear all tabs).............. Ctrl + End
7. Place cursor at designated location for tab setting.
8. Select from one of the following tab styles:............**Option**

   a) Select **L** (Left justify text [default setting])
   b) Select **R** (Right justify text)
   c) Select **D** (Decimal align text)
   d) Select **C** (Center text)
   e) Select **L** (Left justify text, preceded by dot leader)
   f) Select **R** (Right justify text, preceded by dot leader)
   g) Select **D** (Decimal align text, preceded by dot leader)
   h) Select **C** (Center text, preceded by dot leader)

   NOTE: Type a period (.) over the letter for those tabs that require a dot leader. They will be displayed in in reverse video .

9. Repeat steps 7 and 8 for all tabs.

   NOTE: A tab can be deleted by moving cursor under the tab style and pressing the delete key.

10. Press **F7**.. F7
11. Press **F7** (return to document)................................... F7

continued...

MULTIPLE TABS SET AT REPEATED INTERVALS

1. Press **Shift + F8** (Format menu)................ Shift + F8
2. Select **L** (Line format).. L
3. Select **T** (Tab set).. T
4. Press **Home, Home, Left Arrow**.. Home , Home , ←
5. Press **Ctrl + End** (to clear all tabs).............. Ctrl + End
6. Type position number of first tab.......................... Option
7. Enter.. ↵
8. Type letter of tab style.. Option

   NOTE: See Special tab styles section.

9. Type position number of first tab (again)..............Option
10. Type comma (,).. ,
11. Type number of spaces between tabs.................. Option

    Example: *0,.5 (Will set tabs at every .5 inches beginning at position zero.)*

12. Enter (to set tab intervals)... ↵

    NOTE: A tab can be deleted by moving cursor under tab style and pressing delete.

13. Press **F7** F7
14. Press **F7** (return to document)................................ F7

TAB ALIGN

VERTICALLY LINE UP TEXT OR NUMBERS

1. Press **Ctrl + F6** (Tab Align).......................... Ctrl + F6

   NOTE: "Align Char = ." message appears in the bottom left corner of screen.

2. Type text to be aligned.

   NOTE: The default Align Character is the period (.).

SELECTING SPECIAL ALIGN CHARACTER

1. Press **Shift + F8** (Format menu).............. Shift + F8
2. Select **O** (Other).. O
3. Select **D** (Decimal/Align Character)......................... D
4. Type the alignment character............................ **Option**
5. Enter.. ↵
6. Press **F7** (return to document)................................ F7

INDENT

INDENT FIRST LINE (from left margin)

New paragraph

1. Place cursor at beginning of line.
2. Press **Tab** (until cursor is at appropriate position).... Tab
3. Type paragraph.
4. Enter.. ↵

   NOTE: Change the tabs settings to change the indent values.

Existing paragraph

1. Place cursor on first character of paragraph.
2. Press **Tab** (until cursor is at appropriate position).... Tab

INDENT EVERY LINE OF PARAGRAPH (from left margin)

New paragraph

1. Press **F4** (Indent [until cursor is at correct position]) F4
2. Type paragraph.
3. Enter.. ↵

Existing paragraph

1. Place cursor on first character of paragraph.
2. Press **F4** (Indent [until cursor is at correct position]) F4

continued...

LEFT/RIGHT INDENT

New paragraph

1. Place cursor at beginning of line.
2. Press **Shift + F4** (Indent L/R [until cursor is at appropriate position)]........................ Shift + F4
3. Type text.
4. Enter.. ↵

Existing paragraph

1. Place cursor on first character of paragraph.
2. Press **Shift + F4** (Indent L/R [until cursor is at appropriate position]).......................... Shift + F4

HANGING INDENT

The first line of paragraph begins at left margin, and the remaining lines are indented.

New paragraph

1. Place cursor at beginning of line.
2. Press **F4** (Indent).. F4
3. Press **Shift + Tab** (Margin Release [cursor moves to original position])........... Shift + Tab
4. Type paragraph.
5. Enter.. ↵

Existing paragraph

1. Place cursor on first character in paragraph.
2. Press **F4**.. F4
3. Press **Shift + Tab** (Margin Release)........... Shift + Tab
4. Press Down Arrow.. ↓

LINE SPACING

NOTE: Single spacing is the default.

1. Place cursor at designated location in document for line change.
2. Press **Shift + F8** (Format menu).............. Shift + F8
3. Select **L** (Line).. L
4. Select **S** (Line Spacing)................................ S

   NOTE: Current setting is displayed.

5. Type spacing ....**Option**

   Examples: 1.5 = One and one-half
   2 = Double Space
   3 = Triple Space

6. Enter.. ↵
7. Press **F7** (to return to document)........................ F7

   NOTE: Text after this point will be affected by the spacing change.

CENTERING TEXT

BEFORE TYPING TEXT

1. Place cursor at beginning of line.
2. Press **Shift + F6** (Center)........................ Shift + F6
3. Type text (maximum of one line).
4. Enter .... ↵
5. Repeat steps 1-4 for additional lines.

EXISTING TEXT

NOTE: There must be a Hard Return at the end of he line that will be centered.

1. Place cursor at beginning of line to be centered.
2. Press **Shift + F6** (Center)........................ Shift + F6
3. Press Down Arrow.. ↓

BLOCK OF TEXT

1. Place cursor at beginning of line to be centered.
2. Press **Alt + F4** (Block On)........................... Alt + F4
3. Highlight text. (See Block Text section.)
4. Press **Shift + F6** (Center)........................ Shift + F6
5. Select **Y** (to center highlighted text)....................... Y

continued...

CENTERING A PAGE FROM TOP TO BOTTOM

1. Place cursor at beginning of page to centered
2. Press **Shift + F8** (Format menu)................ Shift + F8
3. Select **P** (Page menu).. P
4. Select **C** (Center page top to bottom)........................ C
5. Press **F7** (Exit Page menu).. F7

NOTE: The text will not appear centered on the screen, but will print with text centered vertically.

CENTER A HEADING IN A COLUMN

1. Place cursor at the beginning of the column.
2. Press **Shift + F6** (Center)........................... Shift + F6
3. Type text.
4. Enter... ↵

UNDERLINING TEXT

BEFORE TYPING TEXT

1. Press **F8** (Underline) F8
2. Type text.
3. Press **F8** (Underline) F8

EXISTING TEXT

1. Place cursor on first character to be underlined.
2. Press **Alt + F4** (Block on)................................ Alt + F4
3. Highlight text. (See Block Text section.)
4. Press **F8** (Underline).. F8

continued...

DOUBLE UNDERLINE NEW TEXT

1. Press **Ctrl + F8** (Font menu)........................ Ctrl + F8
2. Select **A** (Appearance).. A
3. Select **D** (Double Underline)................................... D
4. Type text.
5. Press Right Arrow.. →

DOUBLE UNDERLINE EXISTING TEXT

1. Place cursor on first character to be underlined.
2. Press **Alt + F4** (Block on)............................ Alt + F4
3. Highlight text. (See Block Text section.)
4. Press **Ctrl + F8** (Font) .... Ctrl + F8
5. Select **A** (Appearance).. A
6. Select **D** (Double Underline)................................... D

UNDERLINING SPACES/TABS

1. Press **Shift + F8** (Format menu)............... Shift + F8
2. Select **O** (Other).. O
3. Select **U** (Underline).. U
4. Make selections.
5. Press **F7** (return to document)............................. F7

JUSTIFICATION ON/OFF

1. Place cursor at location for justification change.
2. Press **Shift + F8** (Format menu) .... Shift + F8
3. Select **L** (Line).. L
4. Select **J** (Justification) .... J
5. Select justification setting:
   a) Select **Y** (yes).. Y
      or OR
   b) Select **N** (no).. N
6. Press **F7** (return to document).................................. F7

FLUSH RIGHT

To align text flush against the right margin.

BEFORE TYPING TEXT

1. Press **Alt + F6** (Flush Right)........................ Alt + F6

   NOTE: Cursor moves to the right margin.

2. Type text (maximum of one line).
3. Enter .... ↵
4. Repeat steps 1-3 for additional lines.

EXISTING TEXT

NOTE: There must be a Hard Return at the end of the line that will be made flush right.

1. Place cursor at beginning of text to be made flush right.
2. Press **Alt + F4** (Block On)............................ Alt + F4
3. Highlight text. (See Block Text section.)
4. Press **Alt + F6** (Flush Right)........................ Alt + F6
5. Select **Y** .... Y

BOLDING TEXT

BEFORE TYPING TEXT

1. Press **F6** (Bold).. F6
2. Type text.
3. Press **F6** (Bold).. F6

EXISTING TEXT

1. Place cursor at beginning of text to be bolded.
2. Press **Alt + F4** (Block on)............................ Alt + F4
3. Highlight text. (See Block Text section.)
4. Press **F6** (Bold).. F6

MOVE AND COPY TEXT

BLOCK OF TEXT

1. Place cursor on first character of text to be moved or copied.
2. Press **Alt + F4** (Block on) .... Alt + F4
3. Highlight text. (See Block Text section.)
4. Press **Ctrl + F4** (Move menu)...................... Ctrl + F4
5. Select **B** (Block).. B
6. Select **M** (Move).. M

   or ... OR

   Select **C** (Copy)... C
7. Place cursor where text is to be retrieved.
8. Enter.. ↵

continued...

SENTENCE/PARAGRAPH/PAGE

1. Place cursor on first character of text to be moved or copied.
2. Press **Ctrl + F4** (Move menu) .... Ctrl + F4
3. Select one of the following options: **Option**
   a) Select **S** (Sentence).................................... S
   b) Select **P** (paragraph).................................... P
   c) Select **A** (Page) .... A
4. Select **M** (Move).................................... M
   or OR
   Select **C** (Copy) C
5. Place cursor where text is to be retrieved.
6. Enter.................................... ↵

continued...

TABULAR COLUMN/RECTANGULAR BLOCK OF TEXT

1. Place cursor on first character of text to be moved or copied.
2. Press **Alt + F4** (Block on)............................ Alt + F4
3. Highlight text. (See Block Text section.)
4. Press **Ctrl + F4** (Move menu)...................... Ctrl + F4
5. Select **C** (Tabular Column)................................. C

   or OR

   Select **R** (Rectangle).. R
6. Select **M** (Move).. M

   or OR

   Select **C** (Copy)... C
7. Place cursor where text is to be retrieved.
8. Enter.. ↵

EXTERNAL COPY

To copy text from one document to another. The original document and its target must already be saved. (See Saving A Document section).

1. Clear Screen (see Clear Screen section).
2. Press **Shift + F1O** (Retrieve).................. Shift + F10
3. Type name of source document.......................... **Option**
4. Enter.. ↵
5. Place cursor on first character of text to be copied.
6. Press **Alt + F4** (Block on)............................ Alt + F4
7. Highlight text. (See Block Text section.)
8. Press **Ctrl + F4** (Move menu)..................... Ctrl + F4
9. Select **B** (Block).. B
10. Select **C** (Copy).. C
11. Press **F7**... F7
12. Enter .... ↵
13. Enter... ↵
14. Select **Y** .... Y
15. Enter... ↵
16. Retrieve target document.
17. Place cursor at designated location where text is to be retrieved.
18. Enter... ↵

APPEND

To add a block of text to the end of an existing document.

1. Place cursor on first character of text to be appended.
2. Press **Alt + F4** (Block on)............................ Alt + F4
3. Highlight text. (See Block Text section.)
4. Press **Ctrl + F4** (Move menu)...................... Ctrl + F4
5. Select **B** (Block).. B
6. Select **A** (Append)... A
7. Type name of document to which block will be appended...**Option**
8. Enter.. ↵

PAPER SIZE/TYPE

1. Place cursor at top of page where new settings are to begin.
2. Press **Shift + F8** (Format menu)................ **Shift** + **F8**
3. Select **P** (Page).. **P**
4. Select **S** (Paper Size).. **S**
5. Select from one of the following Page Sizes: **Option**
   a) Select **S** (Standard) 8.5" x 11"............................ **S**
   b) Select **T** (Standard Landscape) 11" x 8.5"......... **T**
   c) Select **L** (Legal) 8.5" x 14"................................. **L**
   d) Select **G** (Legal Landscape) 14" x 8.5"............... **G**
   e) Select **E** (Envelope) 9.5" x 4"............................. **E**
   f) Select **H** (Half Sheet) 5.5" x 8.5"......................... **H**
   g) Select **U** (US Government) 8" x 11".................. **U**
   h) Select **A** (A4) 210mm x 297mm.......................... **A**
   i) Select **N** (A4 Landscape) 297mm x 210mm....... **N**
   j) Select **O** (Other)... **O**
6. Select from one of the following Types: **Option**
   a) Select **S** (Standard).. **S**
   b) Select **B** (Bond) .... **B**
   c) Select **H** (Letterhead).. **H**
   d) Select **L** (Labels)... **L**
   e) Select **E** (Envelope).. **E**
   f) Select **T** (Transparency)...................................... **T**
   g) Select **C** (Cardstock).. **C**
   h) Select **O** (Other).. **O**

   NOTE: The Size and Type are compared with the forms in the form menu. If they do not match, then WordPerfect substitutes with its own form. See Creating Forms for more information.

7. Press **F7** (return to document)................................ **F7**

PAGE NUMBERING

1. Place cursor at top of page to be numbered.
2. Press **Shift + F8** (Format menu)............... Shift + F8
3. Select **P** (Page)... P
4. Select **P** (Page Numbering)................................... P
5. Select one of the following options: **Option**
   a) Select **1** (Print on top left of every page)............ 1
   b) Select **2** (Print on top center of every page)....... 2
   c) Select **3** (Print on top right of every page)........... 3
   d) Select **4** (Print on top, alternating left and right on every page)... 4
   e) Select **5** (Print on bottom left of every page)....... 5
   f) Select **6** (Print on bottom center of every page).. 6
   g) Select **7** (Print bottom right of every page).......... 7
   h) Select **8** (Print on bottom, alternating left and right).. 8
   i) Select **N** (No page numbers)................................ N
6. Press **F7** (return to document)................................ F7

NEW PAGE NUMBER

1. Place cursor at top of page to be renumbered.
2. Press **Shift + F8** (Format menu)................ Shift + F8
3. Select **P** (Page).. P
4. Select **N** (New page number).................................. N
5. Type new page number....................................... **Option**
6. Enter.. ↵
7. Press **F7** (return to document)................................ F7

CONDITIONAL END OF PAGE

To protect a certain number of lines from being split by a page break.

1. Place cursor on the line above the text to be kept together.
2. Press **Shift + F8** (Format menu)............... Shift + F8
3. Select **O** (Other)... O
4. Select **C** (Conditional End of Page).......................... C
5. Type the number of lines to be kept together.......**Option**
6. Enter.. ↵
7. Press **F7** (return to document)................................ F7

HARD PAGE BREAK

INSERT

1. Place cursor where new page is to begin.
2. Press **Ctrl + Enter**... Ctrl + ↵

NOTE: A Hard Page break is displayed as a line of equal signs (=).

DELETE

1. Place cursor immediately after the Hard Page break line.
2. Press **backspace** (to delete Hard Page break)....................................... Backspace

BLOCK PROTECT

To protect a block of text from being separated by a soft page break.

1. Place cursor on first character of text to be protected by a soft page break.
2. Press **Alt + F4** (Block on)............................ Alt + F4
3. Highlight text. (See Block Text section.)
4. Press **Shift + F8** (Format menu)............... Shift + F8

   NOTE: "Protect block? (Y/N)" message appears at the bottom left of screen.

5. Select **Y** (to protect highlighted text)........................ Y

WIDOW/ORPHAN PROTECTION ON/OFF

1. Place cursor at beginning of document where text will be protected from widows and orphans.
2. Press **Shift + F8** (Format menu)............... Shift + F8
3. Select **L** (Line).. L
4. Select **W** (Widow/Orphan Protection)....................... W
5. Select Widow/Orphan setting:

   a) Select **Y** (turn on).. Y

   or OR

   b) Select **N** (turn off)... N

6. Press **F7** (return to document)................................ F7

HARD SPACE

To keep two or more words together on the same line; such as a name, a date, or an equation.

1. Type the first word..**Option**
2. Press **Home + Spacebar** (Hard Space)............................ **Home** + **Spacebar**
3. Type the next word..**Option**

HYPHENATION

TURNING HYPHENATION ON

1. Place cursor where hyphenation is to begin.
2. Press **Shift + F8** (Format menu)............... **Shift** + **F8**
3. Select **L** (Line).. **L**
4. Select **Y** (Hyphenation)..................................... **Y**
5. Select the hyphenation setting:
   a) Select **M** (Manual)...................................... **M**
   or .... OR
   b) Select **A** (Auto)... **A**
6. Press F7 (return to document)............................... **F7**

   NOTE: When a word needs to be hyphenated, a beep will sound and the message "Position hyphen; Press ESC" will appear at bottom of screen.

7. Press **Left** or **Right Arrow**...................... **←** OR **→**
8. Press **Escape** (to hyphenate word)........................ **Esc**

continued...

TURNING HYPHENATION OFF

1. Place cursor where hyphenation is to end.
2. Press **Shift + F8** (Format menu)............... Shift + F8
3. Select **L** (Line).. L
4. Select **Y** (Hyphenation).. Y
5. Select **F** (Off).. F
6. Press **F7** (return to document)................................ F7

SETTING H-ZONE

NOTE: The H-Zone determines if a word should be hyphenated or wrapped to the next line when the hyphenation feature is on. The H-Zone is preset to 7 and 0.

1. Press **Shift + F8** (Format menu)............... Shift + F8
2. Select **L** (Line).. L
3. Select **Z** (Set the H-Zone)...................................... Z
4. Type the percentage for the left zone.................. **Option**
5. Enter.. ↵
6. Type the percentage for the right zone................ **Option**
7. Enter.. ↵
8. Press **F7** (return to document)................................ F7

NOTE: A smaller H-Zone requires more hyphenation. A large H-Zone requires less hyphenation.

CASE CONVERSION

Change an existing block of text to upper or lower case.

1. Place cursor at beginning of text for case conversion.
2. Press **Alt + F4** (Block on)............................ Alt + F4
3. Highlight text. (See Block Text section.)
4. Press **Shift + F3** (Case Conversion menu).. Shift + F3
5. Select **U** (Uppercase).. U

   or OR

   Select **L** (Lowercase).. L

CAPITALIZATION

1. Press **Caps-Lock key** (UPPER CASE)....... Caps Lock

   NOTE: "Pos" changes to "POS" on the status line.

2. Type text to be in UPPER CASE.
3. Press **Caps-Lock key** (End UPPER CASE) Caps Lock

   NOTE: "POS" changes back to "Pos" on the status line.

COLUMNS

CREATE

1. Press **Alt + F7** (Math/Columns menu)............ Alt + F7
2. Select **D** (Column Definition).................................. D
3. Select **T** (Type).. T
4. Select the appropriate type of column: **Option**
   a) Select **N** (Newspaper).. N
   b) Select **P** (Parallel)... P
   c) Select **B** (Parallel with block protect).................... B
5. Select **N** (Number of Columns)................................ N
6. Type number .... **Option**

   NOTE: Maximum of 24 columns.
7. Enter.. ↵

   NOTE: To create columns of unequal margins
   a) Select **M** (Margins)... M
   b) Enter new margins.
8. Press **F7** (to accept columns setting)...................... F7
9. Select **C** (Column On/Off).. C

   NOTE: "Col 1" is added to the status line.
10. Type column text.

    NOTE: To end a column, press Ctrl + Enter (Hard Page break). Cursor will move to the top of the next column.
11. Repeat step 10 for all columns.

continued...

TURN COLUMNS OFF

1. Press **Alt + F7** (Math/Columns menu).......... Alt + F7
2. Select **C** (Column On/Off).. C

   NOTE: "Col" disappears from status line.

EDITING COLUMNS

Cursor Movements Within a column using the Go To Key (Ctrl +Home)

To Previous Column......................... Ctrl + Home , ←

To the Next Column......................... Ctrl + Home , →

To the First Column........... Ctrl + Home , Home , ←

To the Last Column........... Ctrl + Home , Home , →

MOVE/COPY TEXT WITHIN A COLUMN

NOTE: Use the Block feature to Move or Copy text.

COLUMN DISPLAY ON/OFF

Display each column on a separate page instead of side-by-side.

1. Retrieve document which contains columns.
2. Press **Shift + F1** (Setup)........................... Shift + F1
3. Select **D** (Display).. D
4. Select **S** (Side-by-Side Columns Display)............ S
5. Select **N** (Turn Off Display)..................................... N

   or OR

   Select **Y** (Turn On Display)..................................... Y
6. Press **F7** (return to document)............................. F7

   NOTE: Every column within every document will henceforth be displayed appropriately by the change.

HEADERS/FOOTERS

CREATE

NOTE: There can be two headers and two footers in a document.

1. Place cursor at the beginning of page where header is to begin.
2. Press **Shift + F8** (Format menu)............... Shift + F8
3. Select **P** (Page)... P
4. Select **H** (Headers)... H

   or OR

   Select **F** (Footers).. F
5. *Select the type of header:*
   a) Select **A** (Header A)... A

      or OR

   b) Select **B** (Header B)... B

      or OR

   Select the type of footer:

   a) Select **A** (Footer A)... A

      or OR

   b) Select **B** (Footer B)... B
6. Select how often header or footer will occur: **Option**
   a) Select **P** (Every Page)...................................... P
   b) Select **O** (Odd Pages)....................................... O
   c) Select **V** (Even Pages)...................................... V
7. Type header or footer.
8. Press **F7** (exit header and return to format menu)... F7
9. Press **F7** (return to document)............................ F7

   NOTE: The header or footer is not visible on the screen. Press Alt + F3 (Reveal Codes) to view the first 50 characters of text.

continued...

EDIT

NOTE: WordPerfect searches "backward" through the text to find the header or footer to edit.

1. Press **Shift + F8** (Format menu) .... Shift + F8
2. Select **P** (Page) .... P
3. Select **H** (Headers) .... H

   or .... OR

   Select **F** (Footer) .... F
4. Select the type of header:

   a) Select **A** (Header A) .... A

   or .... OR

   b) Select **B** (Header B) .... B

   or .... OR

   Select the type of footer:

   a) Select **A** (Footer A) .... A

   or .... OR

   b) Select **B** (Footer B) .... B
5. Select **E** (Edit) .... E
6. Edit header or footer.
7. Press **F7** F7
8. Press **F7** (return to document) F7

FOOTNOTES/ENDNOTES

CREATE

1. Retrieve document for note.
2. Place cursor at the location for note.
3. Press **Ctrl + F7** (Footnote menu)................ Ctrl + F7
4. Select **F** (Footnote).. F

   or OR

   Select **E** (Endnote).. E
5. Select **C** (Create).. C

   NOTE: Number of note appears on top of new screen.
6. Type text.
7. Press **F7** (return to document)................................ F7

   NOTE: Note number appears in document and will print in subscript. Text of note will <u>not</u> appear on screen. Press Reveal Codes (Alt + F3) to see note.

continued...

EDIT

1. Retrieve document with note to be edited.
2. Press **Ctrl + F7** (Footnote menu)................ Ctrl + F7
3. Select **F** (Footnote).. F

   or OR

   Select **E** (Endnote).. E
4. Select **E** (Edit).. E
5. Type the number of the note to be edited............**Option**
6. Enter.. ↵
7. Edit note.
8. Press **F7** (return to document)................................ F7

DELETE

1. Place cursor on note number to be deleted.
2. Press **Delete**.. Del
3. Select **Y** (to confirm deletion).................................. Y

NOTE: Remaining notes in document are automatically renumbered.

MATH

DEFINING COLUMNS

1. Set Tabs (see Tab Set section).
2. Press **Alt + F7** (Math/Columns menu)........... Alt + F7
3. Select **E** (Math Definition menu)............................. E
4. Define column type: **Option**
   a) Select **0** (Calculation)....................................... 0
   b) Select **1** (Text).. 1
   c) Select **2** (Numeric).. 2
   d) Select **3** (Total).. 3

When option **0** (Calculation) is selected

Type desired formula for the column.

	Formula	Result
Example:	2*3-1/2	2.50

*NOTE: There are four operators used to create a formula + add, - subtract, * multiply,/ divide.*

5. Enter.. ↵
6. Repeat steps 4 and 5 to define other columns.

NOTE: A maximum of four calculation columns can be created.

7. Press **F7**.. F7
8. Press **F7** (return to document)................................ F7

continued...

CALCULATIONS WITHIN A DOCUMENT

1. Set Tabs (see Tab Set section).
2. Press **Alt + F7** (Math/Columns menu)............ Alt + F7
3. Select **M** (Math on)... M

   NOTE: Math message appears at the bottom of screen.

4. Type numbers to be calculated:

   a) **Tab** (to numeric column).................................... Tab

   b) Type number to be calculated.........................**Option**

   NOTE: An ! (formula operator) will appear in the calculation column. Do not enter numbers in a calculation column.

   c) Repeat steps a and b for each "math" column.

   d) Enter (to move to next line)................................ ↵

   e) Follow steps a-c for each column of numbers to be calculated.

   NOTE: To indicate a negative number use a negative sign, parentheses or "N" operator.

   Example: *-3.40 or (3.40) or N3.40.*

continued...

Math (continued)

5. To calculate:

A SUBTOTAL

a) Enter (to move to next line)............................ ↵

b) **Tab** (to bottom of numeric column to be calculated).. Tab

c) Type **+** (to create subtotal)................................ +

d) Follow steps b-c for all columns to be calculated.

e) Press **Alt + F7** (Math/Columns menu)... Alt + F7

f) Select **A** (Calculate).. A

A TOTAL

To add subtotals

a) Enter (to move to next line)............................ ↵

b) **Tab** (to bottom of numeric column to be calculated)

c) Type = (to create total).................................... =

d) Follow steps b-c for all columns to be calculated.

e) Press **Alt + F7** (Math/Columns menu).. Alt + F7

f) Select **A** (calculate).. A

continued...

A GRAND TOTAL

To add a number to an existing total.

a) Enter (to move to next line)................................ ↵

b) **Tab** (to numeric column to be calculated).......... Tab

c) Type **T**.. T

d) Type number to be calculated..........................**Option**
Example T2000.00

e) Repeat steps b-d for all columns to be calculated.

f) Press Enter twice to add extra spacing.... ↵ , ↵

g) **Tab** (to bottom of numeric column
to be calculated).. Tab

h) Type * (to create grand total)............................ *

i) Repeat steps g-h for all columns to be calculated.

j) Press **Alt + F7** (Math/Columns menu)...... Alt + F7

k) Select **A** (Calculate).. A

continued...

Math (continued)

A CALCULATION COLUMN

a) **Tab** (to calculation column(s))........................... Tab

NOTE: An ! (formula operator) will appear in tthe calculation column. Do not enter numbers in a calculation column.

b) Press **Alt + F7** (Math/Columns menu)..... Alt + F7

c) Select **A** (Calculate)... A

NOTE: The result of calculation column will be displayed.

TURN MATH OFF

1. Press **Alt + F7** (Math/Column menu)............ Alt + F7
2. Select **M** (Math Off).. M

*NOTE: The operators (+, =, T, *, etc.) from the math appear on the screen but do not print.*

MERGE

CREATE A SECONDARY FILE (Data File)

NOTE: A Record contains a group of related fields. A record may contain information on a particular person or item.

A field is a single element in a record. A field may contain for example a title, first name or last name.

1. Clear screen (see Clear Screen section).
2. Type the data for the first merge field.
3. Press **F9** (^R code).. F9
4. Repeat steps 1-2 for each field in the record.

   NOTE: If a field within a record is blank Press F9 (^R). This holds a place for the field. (See illustration on the following page.)

5. Press **Shift + F9** (Merge Codes) at record end.. Shift + F9
6. Select **E** (end of record).. E

   NOTE: This will also insert a page break.

7. Repeat steps 2-6 to enter additional records.

continued...

Merge (continued)

Create a Secondary File (Data File continued)

8. Press **F7**.. F7
9. Enter.. ↵
10. Type name of document.. **Option**

    NOTE: Use the extension .sf when naming the document to identify the file as a secondary file. ***Example:*** *letter.sf*

11. Enter .... ↵
12. Enter.. ↵

Example:

Without a blank field		**With a blank field**
Mr.^R		Ms.^R
Anthony^R		^R
Salazar^R	or	Richardson^R
Marketing Dept^R		^R
DDC^R		DDC^R
14 East 38th St ^R		14 East 38th St ^R
New York^R		New York^R
NY^R		NY^R
10016^R		10016^R
^E		^E

CREATE A PRIMARY FILE

NOTE: Each field in a record is numbered
Example: *F1=Title*
F2=First name

1. Clear screen (see Clear Screen section).
2. Place cursor where field is to be placed.
3. Press **Shift + F9** (Merge Codes)............. Shift + F9
4. Select **F**.. F
5. Type the number of the field.............................. **Option**
6. Enter.. ↵
7. Repeat steps 2-6 for each additional merge field.
8. Type in remainder of document.
9. Press **F7**... F7
10. Enter.. ↵
11. Type name of document................................... **Option**

NOTE: Use the extension .pf when naming the document to identify file as a primary file. ***Example:*** *letter.pf*

13. Enter.. ↵
14. Enter.. ↵

Example:

Primary File	**Merged Record**
^F1^ ^F2^ ^F3^	Mr. Anthony Salazar
^F4^	Marketing Dept
^F5^	Dictation Disc Co.
^F6^	14 East 38th Street
^F7^, ^F8^ ^F9^	New York, NY 10016
Dear ^F1^ ^F3^:	Dear Mr. Salazar:
Thank you, ^F1^ ^F3^, for	Thank you, Mr. Salazar, for

continued

TO ELIMINATE BLANK LINES IN A RECORD

NOTE: Only use when a field represents a complete line.

1. Press **Shift + F9** (Merge Codes)................ Shift + F9
2. Select **F**.. F
3. Type field number of the blank line..................... **Option**
4. Type a question mark (?) after the field number....... ?
5. Enter.. ↵

Example: ^F4?^

NOTE: If a field is blank in the secondary File, the question mark prevents a blank line from appearing in the merged document.

Example (with a blank line):

Primary File	**Merged Record**
^F1^ ^F2^ ^F3^	Ms. Richardson
^F4?^	Dictation Disc Co.
^F5^	14 East 38th St
^F6^	New York, NY 10016
^F7^, ^F8^ ^F9^	
Dear ^F1^ ^F3^:	Dear Ms. Richardson:
Thank you, ^F1^ ^F3^, for	Thank you, Ms. Richardson, for

continued...

CREATE A MERGED DOCUMENT

1. Press **Ctrl + F9** (Merge/Sort menu).............. Ctrl + F9
2. Select **M** (Merge)... M
3. Type the name of the primary file........................ Option
4. Enter.. ↵
5. Type the name of the secondary file.................... Option
6. Enter.. ↵

NOTE: The merged document will appear on screen.

SAVE MERGED DOCUMENT

1. Press **F7**.. F7
2. Enter.. ↵
3. Type name of document.. Option
4. Enter.. ↵
5. Enter.. ↵

NOTE: To print document see Print section.

continued...

ENVELOPES (Primary File)

NOTE: The example shows the steps for hand-feeding envelopes (9" X 4").

1. Clear screen (see Clear Screen section).
2. Press **Shift + F8** (Format menu)................ Shift + F8
3. Select **P** (Page).. P
4. Select **S** (Size/Type).. S
5. Select **E** (Envelopes Paper Size).......................... E
6. Select **E** (Envelopes Paper Type).......................... E

   *NOTE: If the form does not exist (designated by *'s) then it must be created. See FORMS section.*

7. Press **F7** (return to document)................................ F7
8. Press **Shift + F8** (Format menu)................ Shift + F8
9. Select **L** (Line).. L
10. Select **M** (Margins Left/Right)................................ M
11. Type **4.5** (left margin).. 4.5
12. Enter.. ↵
13. Type **0** (right margin).. 0
14. Enter.. ↵
15. Enter.. ↵
16. Select **P** (Page).. P
17. Select **M** (Margins Top/Bottom)................................ M
18. Type **0** (top margin)... 0
19. Enter.. ↵
20. Type **0** (bottom margin).. 0

continued...

Envelopes (Primary File continued)

21. Enter.. ↵
22. Enter.. ↵
23. Select **O** (Other).. O
24. Select **A** (Advance).. A
25. Select **D** (Down)... D
26. Type **1.5**... 1.5
27. Enter.. ↵
28. Press **F7** (return to document)...................................... F7
29. Repeat steps 2-7 of Create a Primary File (to place the name and address lines).

Example:

Primary File	**Merged Record**
^F1^ ^F2^ ^F3^	Mr. Stuart Auslander
^F4^	Riverdale Shipping
^F5^	121 Mariners Drive
^F6^, ^F7^ ^F8^	Spring, ME 01342

---

30. Press **F7** F7
31. Enter.. ↵
32. Type name of document.. **Option**

    Example: Envelope.pf

33. Enter.. ↵
34. Enter.. ↵

continued...

TO CREATE A SECONDARY FILE

See Create a Secondary File section.

CREATE A MERGED DOCUMENT FOR PRINTING ENVELOPES

See Create a Merge Document section.

SAVE MERGED ENVELOPE

1. Press **F7**.. F7
2. Enter.. ↵
3. Type name of document.................................... **Option**

   Example: Envelopes

4. Enter.. ↵
5. Enter.. ↵

   NOTE: To print document see Printing A Document.

continued...

SINGLE WIDTH LABELS (Primary File)

NOTE: The example displays the steps for 4" X 1 + 7/16" labels.

1. Clear screen (see Clear Screen section).
2. Press **Shift + F8** (Format menu)............. Shift + F8
3. Select **L** (Line).. L
4. Select **M** (Margins)..................................... M
5. Type **.5** (left margin)................................. .5
6. Enter... ↵
7. Type **0** (right margin)................................ 0
8. Enter... ↵
9. Enter... ↵
10. Select **P** (Page)...................................... P
11. Select **M** (Margins Top/Bottom).......................... M
12. Type **0** (top margin)................................. 0
13. Enter.. ↵
14. Type **0** (bottom margin).............................. 0
15. Press **F7** (return to document).......................... F7
16. Press **Shift + F8** (Format menu).............. Shift + F8
17. Select **P** (Page)....................................... P
18. Select **S** (Page Size/Type)............................. S
19. Select **0** (Paper Size)................................. 0
20. Type **4** (width).. 4
21. Enter.. ↵
22. Type **1.44** (length).................................. 1.44

continued...

Single width labels (Primary File continued)

23. Enter.. [Enter]
24. Select **L** (Labels)..................................... [L]
25. Press **F7** (return to document)...................... [F7]
26. Repeat steps 2-7 of Create a Primary File (to mark the placement of the name and address lines)
27. Press **F7** .... [F7]
28. Enter.. [Enter]
29. Type name of document.................................**Option**

    Example: Labels.pf

30. Enter.. [Enter]
31. Enter.. [Enter]

SINGLE WIDTH LABELS (Secondary File)

See Create a Secondary File section.

TO CREATE A MERGE DOCUMENT FOR SINGLE-WIDTH LABELS.

See Create a Merge Document section.

SAVE MERGED LABEL

1. Press **F7**.. [F7]
2. Enter.. [Enter]
3. Type name of document.................................**Option**

   Example: Labels

4. Enter.. [Enter]
5. Enter.. [Enter]

NOTE: To print document see Printing A Document.

continued...

MULTIPLE WIDTH LABELS (Primary File)

NOTE: The example settings show the format for an 8 +1/2" X 11" sheet triple-width labels.

1. Clear screen (see Clear Screen section).
2. Press **Shift + F8** (Format menu)............... Shift + F8
3. Select **P** (Page)............... P
4. Select **M** (Margins Top/Bottom)............... M
5. Type **.25** (top margin)............... .25
6. Enter............... ↵
7. Type **.25** (bottom margin)............... .25
8. Enter............... ↵
9. Enter............... ↵
10. Enter............... ↵
11. Press **Alt + F7** (Math/Columns menu)............... Alt + F7
12. Select **D** (Columns Def)............... D
13. Select **T** (Type)............... T
14. Select **B** (Parallel with Block Protect)............... B
15. Select **N** (Number of Columns)............... N
16. Type **3**............... 3
17. Enter............... ↵
18. Select **M** (Margins)............... M
19. Type **.25** (left margin of first column)............... .25
20. Enter............... ↵
21. Type **3** (right margin of column)............... 3
22. Enter............... ↵

continued...

Merge (continued)

Multiple width labels (Primary File continued)

23. Type **3** (left margin of second column)........................ 3
24. Enter.. ↵
25. Type **5.75** (right margin of second column)............ 5.75
26. Enter.. ↵
27. Type **5.75** (left margin of third column).................. 5.75
28. Enter.. ↵
29. Type **8.25** (right margin of third column)................ 8.25
30. Enter.. ↵
31. Press **F7**.. F7
32. Select **C** (turn column on).. C
33. Place cursor where field is to appear.
34. Press **Shift + F9** (Merge Codes)............... Shift + F9
35. Select **F**... F
36. Type the number of the field to be placed............**Option**
37. Enter.. ↵
38. Repeat steps 33-37 to place the name and address lines.
39. Press **Ctrl + Enter** (end column)................... Ctrl + ↵
40. Press **Shift + F9** (Merge Codes)............... Shift + F9
41. Select **N** .... N
42. Press **Shift + F9** (Merge Codes)............... Shift + F9
43. Select **F**... F
44. Type the number of the field to be placed.......... **Option**
45. Enter.. ↵

continued...

Multiple width labels (Primary File continued)

46. Repeat steps 33-38 (to place the name and address lines in the second column).
47. Press **Ctrl + Enter**.. Ctrl + ↵
48. Repeat steps 33-38 (to place the name and address lines in the third column).
49. Press **Alt + F7** (Math/Columns menu)........... Alt + F7
50. Select **C** (Columns On/Off)..................................... C
51. Press Enter three times .... ↵, ↵, ↵

    NOTE: Vary the number of hard returns if the address is more or less than three lines.

Example:

Primary File

^F1^ ^F2^ ^F3^	^N^F1^ ^F2^ ^F3^	^N^F1^ ^F2^ ^F3^
^F4^	^F4^	^F4^
^F5^	^F5^	^F5^
^F6^	^F6^	^F6^
^F7^, ^F8^ ^F9^	^F7^, ^F8^ ^F9^	^F7^, ^F8^ ^F9^

52. Press **Shift + F9** (Merge Codes)................ Shift + F9
53. Select **N**.. N
54. Press **Shift + F9** (Merge Codes)................ Shift + F9
55. Select **P**.. P

continued...

Merge (continued)

Multiple width labels (Primary File continued)

56. Press **Shift + F9** (Merge codes)................ Shift + F9
57. Select **P**.. P
58. Press **F7**.. F7
59. Enter.. ↵
60. Type name of document..**Option**

    Example labels.pf
61. Enter.. ↵
62. Enter.. ↵

Example:

Primary File

^F1^ ^F2^ ^F3^	^N^F1^ ^F2^ ^F3^	^N^F1^ ^F2^^F3^
^F4^	^F4^	^F4^
^F5^	^F5^	^F5^
^F6^	^F6^	^F6^
^F7^, ^F8^ ^F9^	^F7^, ^F8^ ^F9^	^F7^, ^F8^ ^F9^

^N^P^P

continued...

MULTIPLE WIDTH LABELS (Secondary File)

See Create a Secondary File section.

TO CREATE A MERGE DOCUMENT FOR PRINTING MULTIPLE WIDTH LABELS

See Create a Merged Document section.

SAVE MERGE MULTIPLE WIDTH LABELS

1. Press **F7**.. F7
2. Enter.. ↵
3. Type name of document.................................**Option**
   Example: labels
4. Enter.. ↵
5. Enter.. ↵

NOTE: To print document see Printing A Document.

SEARCH

FORWARD SEARCH

1. Place cursor BEFORE text to be searched.
2. Press **F2** (to display search message).................... F2
3. Type the string of characters and or codes to be searched.
4. Press **F2** (begin search).. F2
5. Edit the text.

   NOTE: The cursor stops after the first match is found.
6. Press **F2** twice (repeat the search)............... F2, F2

   NOTE: Lowercase characters will match both lowercase and UPPERCASE. UPPERCASE will match only UPPERCASE.

continued...

REVERSE SEARCH

1. Place cursor AFTER text to be searched.
2. Press **Shift + F2**.. Shift + F2
3. Type the string of characters and or codes to be searched.
4. Press **Shift + F2** (begin search)................ Shift + F2
5. Edit the text.
6. Press **Shift + F2** twice (to repeat) .... Shift + F2, Shift + F2

EXTENDED SEARCH

NOTE: Extends searching into headers, footers, footnotes, and endnotes.

1. Press **Home**.. Home
2. Press **F2** (Forward Search)...................................... F2
   or OR
   Press **Shift + F2** (Reverse Search)........... Shift + F2
3. Type the string of characters and or codes to be searched.
4. Press **F2** (Forward Search).................................. F2
   or OR
   Press **Shift + F2** (Reverse Search)........... Shift + F2
5. Edit the text.
6. Press **Home**.. Home
7. Press **F2** twice (repeat the search)................ F2, F2
   or OR
   Press **Shift + F2** twice (to repeat).......................... Shift + F2, Shift + F2

REPLACE

1. Press **Alt + F2** (Replace).............................. Alt + F2
2. Select **Y** (to confirm each replacement).................. Y

   or OR

   Enter (to automatically make each replacement)..... ↵
3. Type the string of characters and or codes to be replaced.

   *NOTE: To find a whole word such as **the** (not **the**se, **the**refore, and o**the**r) enter spaces before and after the word.*
4. Press **F2** F2
5. Type the replacement string of characters and or codes.
6. Press **F2** (begin replacing)....................................... F2

   NOTE: If confirmation was selected, each replacement must be individually confirmed or denied.

IN A BLOCK

1. Press **Alt + F4** (Block on).............................. Alt + F4
2. Highlight text. (See Block Text section.)
3. Follow steps 1-6 above to replace.

continued...

SUPER/SUBSCRIPT

NOTE: Printer must support this feature for successful printing.

ONE CHARACTER

1. Place cursor where super/subscript is to be inserted.
2. Press **Ctrl + F8** (Font menu)........................ Ctrl + F8
3. Select **S** (Size).. S
4. Select **P** (Superscript).. P
   or OR
   Select **B** (Subscript)... B
5. Type in text.
6. Press right arrow key (to revert to normal text)........ →

   NOTE: Text will not appear on screen as superscript/subscript but will print appropriately.

BLOCK OF TEXT

1. Press **Alt + F4**.. Alt + F4
2. Highlight text. (See Block Text section.)
3. Press **Ctrl + F8** (Font menu)..................... Ctrl + F8
4. Select **S** (Size).. S
5. Select **P** (Superscript)... P
   or OR
   Select **B** (Subscript)... B

SPELLER

1. Retrieve Document.

   NOTE: If two disk drives, replace the diskette in Drive B with the speller diskette.

2. Press **Ctrl + F2** (begin speller).................... Ctrl + F2

3. Select one of the following from the Check Menu: **Option**

   a) Select **W** (Word).. W
   Check the word on which cursor is blinking.

   b) Select **P** (Page).. P
   Check the page on which cursor is blinking.

   c) Select **D** (Document)...................................... D
   Check the entire document.

   d) Select **N** (New Supplementary Dictionary).......... N
   Use a new supplementary dictionary.

   e) Select **L** (Look up).. L
   Looks up a word in the main dictionary that matches a pattern.

   f) Select **C** (Count).. C
   Counts the words in the document on screen.

   *NOTE: Press **F1** (Cancel key) at any time to stop spell-checking.*

NOT FOUND MENU

*NOTE: When spell-checking using check menu options (**1**-Word, **2**-Page, **3**-Document) misspelled words will appear in reverse video and Not Found Menu will appear at the bottom of screen.*

1. Select one of the following from the Not Found Menu: **Option**

   a) Choose any of the alternative words listed by letter (if any are listed)....................................**Option**

   b) Select **1** (Skip once)... 1
   Speller stops at the next occurrence of the word.

   c) Select **2** (Skip).. 2
   Word is ignored for the rest of the document.

continued...

Speller (continued)

Not Found Menu (continued)

d) Select **3** (Add word).. 3
Word is saved in the supplementary dictionary.

e) Select **4** (Edit).. 4
1) Correct spelling in document.
2) Press **F7**.

f) Select **5** (Look up)... 5
Looks up a word in the main dictionary that matches a pattern, and replaces the misspelled word(s) with the correct spelling.
1) Type word pattern to Look up.
2) Enter.
3) Select letter of correct spelling to replace the misspelled word.

DOUBLE WORD MENU

*NOTE: When spell-checking using menu options (W- Word, **P**-Page, **D**-Document) Double word occurrences will appear in* reverse video *and the Double Word menu will appear at the bottom of screen.*

1. Select one of the following: **Option**

a) Select **1** or **2** (Skip) .... 1 OR 2
Spell-checking continues

b) Select **3** (Delete 2nd).. 3
The second occurrence of the word is deleted.

c) Select **4** (Edit)... 4
1) Manually correct spelling.
2) Press **F7**.

d) Select **5** (Disable Double Word Checking)................ 5
Double words are ignored.

SPELLER UTILITY

NOTE: Creates dictionaries, adds or deletes words, displays the common word list, and checks the location of a word.

Two Disk Drives	**Hard Disk Drive**
At the A> prompt:	At the C> prompt:
1. Place a data diskette in Drive B.	1. Change to WordPerfect directory or other directory that contains spell.exe file.
2. Place the Speller Diskette in Drive A.	2. Type Spell.
3. Type Spell.	3. ENTER.
4. ENTER.	

Select one of the following from the Speller Utility: **Option**

a) Select **0** (Exit) Exit Spell Utility.......................... **0**

b) Select **1** (Change/Create Dictionary)................ **1**
Changes to or creates another dictionary.

c) Select **2** (Add words to dictionary).................... **2**

d) Select **3** (Delete words from dictionary)............ **3**

continued...

Speller Utility (continued)

e) Select **4** (Optimize Dictionary)................................... **4**
Select this after creating new dictionary.

f) Select **5** (Display common list of words)................. **5**

g) Select **6** (Check location of a word)......................... **6**
Checks to see if a word is in the main dictionary or common word list.

h) Select 7 (Look up)... **7**
Check a word pattern.

i) Select **8** (Phonetic Look Up).................................... **8**
Looks up words in the main dictionary that "sound" alike.

j) Select **9** (Convert 4.2 Dictionary to 5.0).................. **9**
Converts 4.2 Dictionary to 5.0

THESAURUS

1. Place cursor on word to be looked up.

   NOTE: If Two Disk Drives, replace the diskette in Drive B with the Thesaurus diskette.

2. Press **Alt + F1** (Thesaurus).......................... **Alt** + **F1**

   NOTE: Press the letter preceding a choice to look up synonyms for that word.

3. Select one of the following from the Thesaurus menu: **Option**

   a) Select **1** (Replace Word)................................ **1**

      1) Press arrow keys to move letters (A,B,C...) to column where word choice is located.
      2) Type the letter preceding the selected word.

Illustration of Screen:

```
select=(v)                 choose=(v)
 1 A ·choose                1    ·cull              choose-(ant)
   B ·cull                       ·pick               5    ·refuse
   C ·designate                  ·select                   ·reject
   D ·pick
   E ·prefer                2    ·adopt
                                 ·embrace
select-(a)                       ·espouse
 2 F ·choice
   G ·elect                 3    ·decide
   H ·elite                      ·determine
   I ·prime                      ·elect
   J ·superior                   ·prefer
```

```
select=(v)                 choose=(v)
1    ·choose                1 A ·cull               choose-(ant)
     ·cull                    B ·pick                5    ·refuse
     ·designate               C ·select                   ·reject
     ·pick
     ·prefer                2 D ·adopt
                              E ·embrace
select-(a)                    F ·espouse
2    ·choice
     ·elect                 3 G ·decide
     ·elite                   H ·determine
     ·prime                   I ·elect
     ·superior                J ·prefer
```

continued...

b) Select **2** (View Document).. **2**

1) Move through document.

2) Press **F7** (return to document).

c) Select **3** (Look Up Word).. **3**

1) Type the word to be looked up.

2) Enter.

d) Select **4** (Clear Column).. **4**

4. Press **F7** (Exit and return to document)

ARROW KEYS

To Move Within the Thesaurus columns:

1. Press right or left arrow to move to another column and choose its letter choices for a replacement.. → OR ←

2. Press up arrow or down arrow to view any subgroups that do not fit on the screen..... ↑ OR ↓

OUTLINE

CREATE

1. Create a new document or retrieve document where outline is to be added.

   NOTE: Set Tabs (to determine indent values within outline levels).

2. Place cursor where outline is to begin.
3. Press **Shift + F5** (Date/Outline)................. Shift + F5
4. Select **O** (Outline).. O
5. Enter (to reveal outline level one)............................ ↵

   NOTE: Cursor appears at outline level one.

6. Press **F4** (to indent text).. F4
7. Type text.
8. Enter (to insert next outline number)....................... ↵

continued...

Outline (continued)

9. Press Tab if necessary until the desired outline level is reached.. Tab

Once to reveal level two. ....
→ A.
→ B.
→ etc.

Twice to reveal level three.....................
→ → 1.
→ → 2.
→ → etc.

Three times to reveal level four............
→ → → a.
→ → → b.
→ → → etc.

Four times to reveal level five................
→ → → → (1)
→ → → → (2)
→ → → → etc.

Five times to reveal level six.................
→ → → → → (a)
→ → → → → (b)
→ → → → → etc.

Six times to reveal level seven..............
→ → → → → → i)
→ → → → → → 11
→ → → → → → et

NOTE: Shift + Tab (Margin Release) will move backward through the levels.

continued...

10. Press **F4** (indent).. F4
11. Type text.
12. Repeat steps 8-11 until outline is complete.
13. Press **Shift + F5** (Date/Outline)................. Shift + F5
14. Select **O** (Outline).. O

REMOVING OUTLINE NUMBERS

1. Place cursor on outline number to be edited.
2. Press **Del** (to delete paragraph code) .... Del

NOTE: Remaining outline numbers are automatically renumbered.

continued...

CHANGING OUTLINE NUMBERING STYLES

1. Place cursor where outline style is to change.
2. Press **Shift + F5** (Date/Outline)................ Shift + F5
3. Select **D** (Define).. D
4. Select from the following styles: **Option**
   a) Select **P**.. P
   [Paragraph: 1. a. i. (1) (a) (i) 1) a)]
   b) Select **O**.. O
   [Outline: I. A. 1. a. (1) (a) i) a)]
   c) Select **L**.. L
   [Legal: 1., 1.1, 1.11, etc.]
   d) Select **B**.. B
   [Bullets: •, o, -, ■, *, +,•, x]
   e) Select **U**.. U
   [To create own definition]
5. Press **F7**.. F7
6. Press **F7** (return to document)................................ F7

DATE

TEXT

Computer's "system" date will permanently appear in document.

1. Press **Shift + F5** (Date/Outline)................. Shift + F5
2. Select **T** (Date Text).. T

CODE

Date Code will update daily to computer's "system" date.

1. Press **Shift + F5** (Date/Outline)................. Shift + F5
2. Select **C** (Date Code).. C

LIST FILES

(Use to RETRIEVE, DELETE, RENAME, PRINT, and COPY a document)

1. Press **F5**.. F5

   NOTE: Type drive address if necessary.

2. Enter.. ↵

3. Press arrow keys to highlight document.

4. Select one of the following.................................Option

   a) Select **R** (Retrieve).. R

   b) Select **D** (Delete).. D

      Select **Y** (to confirm deletion)

      NOTE: Once deleted, a document cannot be retrieved.

   c) Select **M** (Move/Rename).................................... M
      1) Type new document name.
      2) Enter.

   d) Select **P** (Print).. P
      1) Type page numbers.
      2) Enter.

      NOTE: Type "Y" if prompted.

   e) Select **C** (Copy)... C
      1) Type name of new document.
      2) Enter.

   f) Press **F7** (return to document).......................... F7

DOCUMENT COMMENTS

To insert a non-printing comment in a document.

CREATE

1. Place cursor where comment is to appear.
2. Press **Ctrl + F5** (Text In/Out menu)............ Ctrl + F5
3. Select **C** (Comment).. C

   NOTE: The Document Comment screen appears with the cursor enclosed in a box.

4. Select **C** (Create).. C
5. Type text of comment.
6. Press **F7** (return to document)............................... F7

   NOTE: Comments cannot be included in a column.

continued...

Document Comments (continued)

EDIT

1. Press **Alt + F3** (Reveal Codes) to verify position in document.................................... Alt + F3
2. Place cursor to the right of comment to be edited.
3. Press **Ctrl + F5** (Text In/Out menu)............ Ctrl + F5
4. Select **C** (Comment)... C
5. Select **E** (Edit)... E
6. Edit comment.
7. Press **F7** (return to document)................................ F7

DISPLAY OF COMMENTS ON/OFF

1. Press **Shift + F1** (Setup)............................ Shift + F1
2. Select **D** (Display)... D
3. Select **D** (Display Document Screen)...................... D
4. Select **N** (No)... N

   or OR

   Select **Y** (Yes)... Y
5. Press **F7** (return to document)................................ F7

   NOTE: Every comment within every document will be displayed appropriately by the change.

REDLINE TEXT

To mark text to be added to document.

1. Retrieve document to be edited.
2. Press **Ctrl + F8** (Font menu)........................ Ctrl + F8
3. Select **A** (Appearance)... A
4. Select **R** (Redline).. R
5. Type text to be Redlined.
6. Press Right Arrow key (end Redline)....................... →

   NOTE: The text is printed with "redline" background.

BLOCK OF TEXT

1. Retrieve document to be edited.
2. Place cursor on first character that will be redlined.
3. Press **Alt + F4** (Block on)............................ Alt + F4
4. Highlight text. (See Block Text section.)
5. Press **Ctrl + F8** (Font menu)........................ Ctrl + F8
6. Select **A** (Appearance)... A
7. Select **R** (Redline).. R

STRIKEOUT TEXT

To mark text to be deleted

1. Retrieve document to be edited.
2. Place cursor on first character that will be struck out.
3. Press **Alt + F4** (Block on)............................ Alt + F4
4. Highlight text. (See Block Text section.)
5. Press **Ctrl + F8** (Font menu)........................ Ctrl + F8
6. Select **A** (Appearance)... A
7. Select **S** (Strikeout).. S

NOTE: When text is printed, each character in the strikeout text is overwritten with a dash.

REMOVE REDLINE AND STRIKEOUT

To delete the Redline markings and Strikeout text.

1. Retrieve document to be edited.
2. Press **Alt + F5** (Date/Outline)....................... Alt + F5
3. Select **G** (Generate).. G
4. Select **R** (Remove Redline and Strikeout).............. R
5. Select **Y** (to delete Redline markings and Strikeout text).. Y

NOTE: Redline codes are deleted. Strikeout text is deleted.

TAB RULER

Use as an editing tool to display current tabs and margin settings for a single document.

1. Retrieve Document
2. Press **Ctrl + F3** (Screen Options)................ Ctrl + F3
3. Select **W** (Window).. W
4. Press Up Arrow .... ↑
5. Enter (to set Tab Ruler in place)............................ ↵

REMOVE TAB RULER

1. Press **Ctrl + F3** (Screen Options)................ Ctrl + F3
2. Select **W** (Window).. W
3. Press Down Arrow (to remove Tab Ruler)............... ↓
4. Enter.. ↵

SPLIT SCREEN (WINDOWS)

To view two documents at once.

NOTE: The Tab Ruler is used to split the screen.

1. Retrieve first document to be edited.
2. Press **Ctrl + F3** (Screen Options)................. Ctrl + F3
3. Select **W** (Window).. W

   NOTE: "# Lines in this Window:24" message appears at the bottom left of screen.

4. Type the number of lines for the current window (any number between 1 and 20).............**Option**

   or OR

   Press Up Arrow to move the Tab Ruler to the correct position... ↑
5. Enter (to set the Window).. ↵
6. Press **Shift + F3** (to move to Doc 2).......... Shift + F3

   NOTE: "Doc 2" appears on the Status Line.

7. Retrieve second document to be edited.
8. Press **Shift + F3**....................................... Shift + F3
   (to move between Doc1 and Doc2)

   NOTE: When switching between documents, the Tab Ruler is updated to reflect the current document settings.

9. Edit documents.

CLOSE WINDOW

1. Press **Ctrl + F3** (Screen Options)............... Ctrl + F3
2. Select **W** (Window)... W
3. Type **24**... 24
4. Enter (to close the Window).................................. ↵

continued...

SAVE AND EXIT DOCUMENT TWO

1. Place cursor in document 2.
2. Press **F7**.. F7
3. Enter.. ↵
4. If the document has been named:

   a) Enter.. ↵

   b) Select **Y** (to replace document).......................... Y

   or OR

   If the document is unnamed:

   a) Type in name..**Option**

   b) Enter.. ↵
5. Select **Y** (Exit second document).......................... Y

SWITCH DOCUMENTS

To edit two documents at the same time

NOTE: Each window is a separate editing screen with its own status line. (See SAVING A DOCUMENT/CLEAR SCREEN Section.)

1. Retrieve first document to be edited.
2. Press **Shift + F3**.. Shift + F3

   NOTE: "Doc 2" appears on the status line indicating second document.

3. Retrieve second document to be edited.
4. Press **Shift + F3**.. Shift + F3
5. Edit documents.

See Save and Exit Document Two for exiting second screen

MACROS

To save a series of keystrokes

CREATE/REPLACE

1. Press **Ctrl + F1O** (Define Macro)................ Ctrl + F10

   NOTE: "Define Macro:" appears on the status line.

2. Type the name of the Macro.................................**Option**
3. Select one of the following options: **Option**

   a) Enter.. ↵

   b) Type full macro name:

      1. Type 1-8 character name............................ **Option**
      2. Press Enter.. ↵

   c) Press **Alt** plus a letter (**A-Z**).

   NOTE: " Macro Def" starts blinking at bottom left of screen.

   *NOTE: If macros exists, Select **R** to replace contents of previous macro or F1 to cancel command.*

4. Type in description of macro (up to 40 characters).
5. Enter.. ↵

   NOTE: Skip steps 4 and 5 if 2a) was chosen.

6. Type keystrokes to be recorded in macro file.
7. Press **Ctrl + F1O** (end macro definition)..... Ctrl + F10

continued...

NOTE: The macro is usually saved in a file on default drive or directory. The file is given an extension of "wpm" by WordPerfect.

PAUSE

Creates a pause in the macro, so variables may be inserted during playback.

1. Follow steps 1-6 in Create/Replace section of macros.
2. Type text until location is reached where pause will occur.
3. Press **Ctrl + PgUp**.................................. Ctrl + PgUp
   (Macro Commands)
4. Select **P** (Pause).. P
5. Continue defining macro.
6. Press **Ctrl + F10**....................................... Ctrl + F10
   (end macro definition)

continued...

PLAYBACK

1. Place cursor where macro is to be executed.
2. Type name of macro:
   a) Press **Alt + F1O** (Start Macro)............ Alt + F10
   b) Type the name of the Macro........................**Option**
   c) Enter.. ↵

NOTE: If a macro was named using the Alt key, press Alt key and letter to execute macro. If macro was created with no name (only a return) then skip step b.

If a pause was created:

1) Type desired text when macro pauses.
2) Enter (continue playback)...................................... ↵

STOPPING MACRO

Press **F1** (Cancel Key) to stop Macro playback............ F1

continued...

EDIT MACRO

1. Press **Ctrl + F1O** (Define macro).............. Ctrl + F10
2. Type the name of existing macro........................ **Option**
3. Enter.. ↵

   NOTE: If a macro was named using the Alt key, skip step 3.

4. Select **E** (Edit).. E
5. Select **D** (Description).. D
6. Edit description.
7. Press **F7**.. F7
8. Select **A** (Action)... A
9. Edit macro commands.

   Note: Pressing Ctrl + PgUp displays the selection of the Macro Commands.

10. Press **F7**.. F7
11. Press **F7** (return to document)................................ F7

ESCAPE

To repeat a character or some functions a specified number of times.

1. Place cursor at location where repetition is to begin.
2. Press **Escape** ("Repeat Value=8" message appears at bottom left of screen)............................ **Esc**
3. Select one of the following features to be repeated: **Option**

   a) Arrow Keys

   b) Delete Word.............................. **Ctrl** + **Backspace**

   c) Delete Line.. **Ctrl** + **End**

   d) Macro.. **Alt** + **F10**

   NOTE: Then type macro name and press ENTER.

   e) Word Left... **Ctrl** + **←**

   f) Word Right... **Ctrl** + **→**

continued...

TO CHANGE REPETITION NUMBER

1. Place cursor where repetition is to begin.
2. Press **Escape** ("Repeat Value=8" message appears at bottom left of screen).......................... **Esc**
3. Type the new number.. **Option**
4. Select the WordPerfect feature (See previous section).

REPEATING A CHARACTER

1. Place cursor where repetition is to begin.
2. Press **Escape** ("Repeat Value=8" message appears at bottom left of screen).......................... **Esc**
3. Type the desired "repetition number".................. **Option**
4. Type the character to be repeated...................... **Option**

LINE DRAW

NOTE: Printer must support this procedure for successful printing.

1. Place cursor where drawing is to begin.
2. Press **Ctrl + F3** (Screen Options)................ Ctrl + F3
3. Select **L** (Line Draw).. L
4. Type number of desired option: **Option**
   a) Select **1** (Single line |)................................ 1
   b) Select **2** (Double line||)................................ 2
   c) Select **3** (Asterisk *)................................ 3
   d) Select **C** (Change) (Additional options).......... C
   e) Select **E** (Erase).. E
   f) Select **M** (Move).. M

   NOTE: By moving the arrow keys without a selection, drawing starts with a single line. Corners are inserted automatically when direction is changed.
5. Use the arrow keys to create the drawing.
6. Press **F7** (Exit Line Draw menu)............................ F7

SORT

SINGLE LINE SORT

1. Press **Ctrl + F9** (Merge/Sort menu)............. Ctrl + F9
2. Select **S** (Sort).. S
3. Type name of document to be sorted.................. **Option**
   (Input file).
4. Enter.. ↵
5. a) Type name of document where sorted
   records are to be saved (Output file)............... **Option**

   b) Enter.. ↵

   or OR

   Enter (to send sorted records to screen).............. ↵
6. Select **T** (Type)... .... T
7. Select **L** (Line).. L
8. Select **K** (Keys).. K
9. Press Delete to delete key definitions after Key1..... Del

   NOTE: The default setting for key1 cannot be deleted

Sort (continued)

Single Line Sort (continued)

10. Define key.

Example:

Key 1 = Type: a (alphanumeric)
Field: 1
Word: 2
or
Key 1 = Type: n (numeric)
Field: 3
Word: 1

Illustration of Screen:

```
------------------------ Sort by Line----------------------------

Key Typ Field Word      Key Typ Field Word      Key Typ Field Word
 1   a     1     2       2                       3
 4                       5                       6
 7                       8                       9
Select

Action                  Order                   Type
Sort                    Ascending               Line sort
```

Illustration of Screen:

```
------------------------ Sort by Line----------------------------

Key Typ Field Word      Key Typ Field Word      Key Typ Field Word
 1   n     3     1       2                       3
 4                       5                       6
 7                       8                       9
Select

Action                  Order                   Type
Sort                    Ascending               Line sort
```

continued...

Single Line Sort (continued)

11. Press **F7** (Exit Keys menu).. F7
12. Select **O** (Order).. O
13. Select **A** (Ascending).. A
    or OR
    Select **D** (Descending)... D
14. Select **P** (Perform Action)....................................... P

    NOTE: To view sorted records saved in a new document (step 5a), retrieve output document.

MULTIPLE LINE SORT

1. Follow Steps 1-9 of Single line sort.
2. Define Keys.

   Example:

   Key 1 = Type: a (alphanumeric)
   Field: 4
   Word: 1

   Key 2 = Type: n (numeric)
   Field: 2
   Word: 1

   Key 3 = Type: a (alphanumeric)
   Field: 1
   Word: 2

NOTE: WordPerfect allows up to 9 keys to be defined.

Illustration of Screen:

```
------------------------Sort by Line------------------------------
Key Typ Field Word    Key Typ Field Word     Key Typ Field Word
 1   a    4     1      2   n    2     1       3   a    1     2
 4                     5                      6
 7                     8                      9
Select

Action                Order                  Type
Sort                  Ascending              Line sort
```

continued...

Sort (continued)

Multiple Line Sort (continued)

3. Press **F7** (Exit Keys menu)........ F7
4. Select **O** (Order)........ O
5. Select **A** (Ascending)........ A

   or .... OR

   Select **D** (Descending)........ D
6. Select **P** (Perform Action)........ P

   NOTE: To view sorted records saved in a new document, retrieve output document.

MERGE SORT (Secondary merge file)

1. Press **Ctrl + F9** (Merge/Sort menu)........ Ctrl + F9
2. Select **S** (Sort)........ S
3. Type name of document to be sorted (Input file)...**Option**
4. Enter........ ↵
5. a) Type name of document where sorted records are to be saved (Output file)........**Option**

   b) Enter........ ↵

   or .... OR

   Enter (to send sorted records to screen)........ ↵
6. Select **T** (Type)........ T
7. Select **M** (Merge)........ M
8. Select **K** (Keys)........ K

continued...

Sort (continued)

Merge Sort (Secondary file,continued)

9. Press Delete to delete key definitions after Key1..... Del

   NOTE: The default setting for key1 cannot be deleted.

10. Define Key(s).

    NOTE: Every ^R defines the end of a field.
    Every ^E defines the end of a record.

Example: Key 1 = Type: n (numeric)
Field: 7
Line: 1
Word: 1

***Illustration of Screen*:**

```
------------------------------ Sort Secondary Merge File -----------------------------
Key Typ Field Line Word  Key Typ Field Line Word  Key Typ Field Line Word
 1   n    7     1    1   2                        3
 4                       5                        6
 7                       8                        9
```

11. Press **F7** (Exit Sort menu).. F7
12. Select **O** (Order).. O
13. Select **A** (Ascending).. A

    or OR

    Select **D** (Descending)... D
14. Select **P** (Perform Action)... P

    NOTE: To view sorted records saved in a new document (step 5a), retrieve output document.

continued...

SELECT ONLY

1. Press **Ctrl + F9** (Merge/Sort menu)............ Ctrl + F9
2. Select **S** (Sort).. S
3. Type name of document to be selected (Input file)..Option
4. Enter.. ↵
5. a) Type name of document where selected records are to be saved (Output file)..........Option

   b) Enter.. ↵

   or OR

   Enter (to send selected records to screen)........... ↵
6. Select **T** (Type).. T
7. Select the type of sort: Option

   a) Select **M** (Merge).. M

   b) Select **L** (Line).. L

   c) Select **P** (Paragraph)...................................... P
8. Select **K** (Keys).. K
9. Press **Delete** to delete key definitions after Key1.... Del

   NOTE: The default setting for key1 cannot be deleted.
10. Define key(s).
11. Press **F7** (Exit Keys menu)..................................... F7
12. Select **S** (Select).. S
13. Press **Ctrl + End** to delete existing select statement(s).. Ctrl + End

continued...

Select Only (continued)

14. Create the select statement.

    Example: Key1=Mr.
    or
    Key1=Hawaii

    NOTE: Select statements can also be created using the following symbols:

+	(OR)	is used to connect two key definitions when either one must be met
*	(AND)	is used to connect two key definitions when both must be met
=		equal to
<>		not equal to
>		greater than
<		less than
>=		greater than or equal to
<=		less than or equal to

Example: key1=Ms.*key2=Smith

15. Press **F7** (Exit Select menu)........ **F7**
16. Select **A** (Action)........ **A**
17. Select **O** (Select Only)........ **O**
18. Select **P** (perform Action)........ **P**

    NOTE: To view selected records saved in a new document (step 5a), retrieve output document.

continued...

GLOBAL SELECT

To request all records containing key words.

1. Follow steps 1-13 of the Select Only (previous) section.
2. Type the select statement using a "g" after the key.

   Example: Keyg=Boston

   NOTE: With "global select" do not type a key number.
3. Press **F7** (Exit Select menu).. F7
4. Select **A** (Action).. A
5. Select **O** (Select Only).. O
6. Select **P** (Perform Action).. P

   NOTE: To view sorted records saved in a new document, retrieve output document.

continued...

SORT AND SELECT (Single and Multiple Line Sort)

1. Press **Ctrl + F9** (Merge/Sort menu)............. Ctrl + F9
2. Select **S** (Sort).. S
3. Type name of document to be sorted (Input file)...**Option**
4. Enter.. ↵
5. a) Type name of document where sorted records are to be saved (Output file)................**Option**

   b) Enter.. ↵

   or OR

   Enter (to send sorted records to screen)............ ↵
6. Select **T** (Type)... T
7. Select **L** (Line).. L
8. Select **K** (Keys)... K
9. Press **Delete** to delete key definitions after Key1.... Del

   NOTE: The default setting for key1 cannot be deleted.

continued...

Sort and Select (Single and Multiple Line Sort) (continued)

10. Define key(s).

    NOTE: Keys must be defined before setting select statement.

11. Press **F7** (Exit Keys menu).. F7
12. Select **S** (Select).. S
13. Press **Ctrl + End** to delete any existing select statement(s).. Ctrl + End
14. Type the select statement. (see step 14 Select Only section)
15. Press **F7** (Exit Select menu).. F7
16. Select **O** (Order).. O
17. Select **A** (Ascending).. A

    or   OR

    Select **D** (Descending).. D
18. Select **A** (Action).. A
19. Select **S** (Select and Sort).. S
20. Select **P** (Perform Action).. P

    NOTE: To view sorted records saved in a new document (step 5a), retrieve output document.

continued...

Sort and Select (Secondary Merge File)

1. Press **Ctrl + F9** (Merge/Sort)........................ Ctrl + F9
2. Select **S** (Sort).. S
3. Type name of document to be sorted (Input file).. **Option**
4. Enter.. ↵
5. a) Type name of document where sorted
   records are to be saved (Output file)............... **Option**

   b) Enter.. ↵

   or OR

   Enter (to send sorted records to screen)............. ↵
6. Select **T** (Type).. T
7. Select **M** (Merge)... M
8. Select **K** (Keys).. K

continued...

Sort (continued)

Sort and Select (Secondary Merge File) (continued)

9. Press **Delete** to delete key definitions after Key1........ Del

   NOTE: The default setting for key1 cannot be deleted.

10. Define Key(s).

    NOTE: Every ^R defines the end of a field.
    Every ^E defines the end of a record.

11. Press **F7** (Exit Sort menu).. F7
12. Select **S** (Select).. S
13. Press **Ctrl + End** to delete any existing select statement(s).. Ctrl + End
14. Type the select statement.
    (See step 14 Select Only section)
15. Press **F7** (Exit Sort menu).. F7
16. Select **O** (Order).. O
17. Select **A** (Ascending).. A

    or OR

    Select **D** (Descending).. D
18. Select **A** (Action).. A
19. Select **S** (Select and Sort)... S
20. Select **P** (Perform Action)... P

    NOTE: To view sorted records saved in a new document (step 5a), retrieve output document.

TABLE OF CONTENTS

A Table of Contents lists topics at the beginning of a document.

1. Retrieve document to have Table of Contents marked.
2. Place cursor on first character to be marked for the Table of Contents.
3. Press **Alt + F4** (Block On)................................ Alt + F4
4. Highlight text. (See Block Text section.)
5. Press **Alt + F5** (Mark Text menu)........................ Alt + F5
6. Select **C** (ToC).. C
7. Type level for Table of Contents................................ Option
8. Repeat steps 2-7 for each item to be included in table.
9. Press **Home + Home + Up Arrow**.. Home + Home + ↑
10. Press **Ctrl + Return**... Ctrl + ↵
11. Press **Left Arrow**.. ←
12. Press **Shift + F6**... Shift + F6
13. Type title of Table of Contents.
14. Press Enter twice.. ↵, ↵
15. Press **Alt + F5** (Mark Text menu)....................... Alt + F5
16. Select **D** (Define)... D
17. Select **C** (Define Table of Contents)............................. C
18. Select **N** (Number of Levels).. N
19. Type in number.. Option
20. Enter.. ↵
21. Press **Alt + F5** (Mark Text menu)...................... Alt + F5
22. Select **G** (Generate)... G
23. Select **G**.. G
24. Enter.. ↵

INDEX (CONCORDANCE)

A concordance index generates page references for selected words in a document.

1. Clear screen (see Clear Screen section).
2. Type the first word(s) for index.
3. Enter.. ↵
4. Repeat steps 2-3 for all words to be included in index.
5. Press **F7**.. F7
6. Enter.. ↵
7. Type name of document (concordance)...............**Option**
8. Enter.. ↵
9. Enter.. ↵
10. Retrieve document to have index created for it.
11. Press **Home+Home+Down Arrow**.. Home + Home + ↓
12. Press **Ctrl + Return**............................ Ctrl + Return
13. Press **Shift + F6**....................................... Shift + F6
14. Type title of index.
15. Press Enter twice... ↵, ↵
16. Press **Alt + F5** (Mark Text menu)............... Shift + F6
17. Select **D** (Define)... D
18. Select **I** (Define Index)..................................... I
19. Type name of concordance document................ **Option**
20. Enter.. ↵

continued...

21. Select Page numbering style: **Option**

    a) Select **N** [No Page Numbers]............................ N

    b) Select **P** [Page Numbers Follow Entries]........... P

    c) Select **(** [(Page Numbers) Follow Entries]......... (

    d) Select **F** [Flush Right Page Numbers].............. F

    e) Select **L** [Flush Right Page Numbers with Leaders]... L

22. Press **Alt + F5** (Mark Text menu)................. Alt + F5

23. Select **G** (Generate).. G

24. Select **G**.. G

25. Enter.. ↵

AUTOMATIC REFERENCE

An automatic reference creates a reference for a target in the document.

1. Place cursor at position where reference will be inserted.
2. Type reference phrase with a space after the last word.

   Example: "See Bar chart, page "
3. Press **Alt + F5** (Mark Text menu)................ Alt + F5
4. Select **R** (Automatic Reference).............................. R
5. Select **R** (Mark Reference).................................... R
6. Select one of the following options: **Option**
   a) Select **P** (Page Number).................................. P
   b) Select **O** (Paragraph/Outline Number).............. O
   c) Select **F** (Footnote Number)................................ F
   d) Select **E** (Endnote Number).............................. E
   e) Select **G** (Graphics Box Number)...................... G
7. Type target name..**Option**
8. Enter.. ↵

   NOTE: A question mark temporarily appears showing where reference number will be.

continued...

Automatic Reference (continued)

9. Place cursor on target.
10. Press **Alt + F5** (Mark Text menu)................ Alt + F5
11. Select **R** (Automatic Reference)............................ R
12. Select **T** (Mark Target).. T
13. Type target name..Option
14. Enter.. ↵
15. Press **Alt + F5** (Mark Text menu)................ Alt + F5
16. Select **G** (Generate).. G
17. Select **G** (Generate Table, Indexes, etc.)............... G
18. Enter.. ↵

FONTS

A font is a family of characters with the same attributes. The selection of fonts depend upon the printer.

CHANGING THE BASE FONT

1. Place cursor at position where font will be changed.
2. Press **Ctrl + F8** (Font menu)........................ Ctrl + F8
3. Select **F** (Base Font).. F
4. Place cursor on font to be selected.
5. Enter...

CHANGING THE SIZE OF BASE FONT

Before typing text

1. Place cursor at position where size of font will be changed.
2. Press **Ctrl + F8** (Font menu)........................ Ctrl + F8
3. Select **S** (Size).. S
4. Select one of the following options: **Option**
   a) Select **P** (Superscript)... P
   b) Select **B** (Subscript).. B
   c) Select **F** (Fine) .... F
   d) Select **S** (Small) .... S
   e) Select **L** (Large) L
   f) Select **V** (Very Large) V
   g) Select **E** (Extra Large)... E

NOTE: The sizes are relative to the base font, and depend on what fonts are available for the printer. If size is unavailable, the closest available size will be substituted.

5. Type in text.
6. Press Right Arrow (turn size change off)................. 

continued...

Changing the Size of Base Font (continued)

Existing text

1. Place cursor at beginning of text where size of font will be changed.
2. Press **Alt + F4** (Block).................................. Alt + F4
3. Highlight text. (See Block Text section.)
4. Press **Ctrl + F8** (Font menu)........................ Ctrl + F8
5. Select **S** (Size).. S
6. Select one of the following options: **Option**
   a) Select **P** (Superscript)....................................... P
   b) Select **B** (Subscript).. B
   c) Select **F** (Fine) .... F
   d) Select **S** (Small) .... S
   e) Select **L** (Large) L
   f) Select **V** (Very Large) V
   g) Select **E** (Extra Large) .... E

   NOTE: The sizes are relative to the base font, and depend on what fonts are available for the printer. If a size is unavailable, the closest available size will be substituted.

continued...

CHANGING THE APPEARANCE OF BASE FONT

Before typing text

1. Place cursor at position where size of font will be changed.
2. Press **Ctrl + F8** (Font menu)........................ Ctrl + F8
3. Select **A** (Appearance)... A
4. Select one of the following options. **Option**
   a) Select **B** (Bold).. B
   b) Select **U** (Underline).. U
   c) Select **D** (Double Underline)............................. D
   d) Select **I** (Italic).. I
   e) Select **O** (Outline)... O
   f) Select **A** (Shadow)... A
   g) Select **C** (Small Caps).. C
   h) Select **R** (Redline)... R
   i) Select **S** (Strikeout)... S

   NOTE: The appearances are relative to the base font, and depend on what fonts are available for the printer. If an appearance is unavailable, the closest available appearance will be substituted.

5. Type in text.
6. Press Right Arrow (turn appearance change off)..... 

continued...

Changing the Appearance of Base Font (continued)

Existing text

1. Place cursor at beginning of text where appearance of font will be changed.
2. Press **Alt + F4** (Block).................................. Alt + F4
3. Highlight text. (See Block Text section.)
4. Press **Ctrl + F8** (Font menu)........................ Ctrl + F8
5. Select **A** (Appearance).. A
6. Select one of the following options: **Option**
   a) Select **B** (Bold).. B
   b) Select **U** (Underline).. U
   c) Select **D** (Double Underline)........................... D
   d) Select **I** (Italic).. I
   e) Select **O** (Outline).. O
   f) Select **A** (Shadow).. A
   g) Select **C** (Small Caps).. C
   h) Select **R** (Redline).. R
   i) Select **S** (Strikeout)... S

NOTE: The appearances are relative to the base font, and depend on what fonts are available for the printer. If an appearance is unavailable, the closest available appearance will be substituted.

PRINT COLOR

NOTE: Print color changes the color of text, and is only available for color printers.

continued...

Fonts (continued)

Print Color (continued)

Changing print color

1. Place cursor at beginning of text where print color will be changed.
2. Press **Ctrl + F8** (Font menu)........................ Ctrl + F8
3. Select **C** (Print Color)........................ C
4. Select one of the following options: **Option**
   a) Select **K** (Black)........................ K
   b) Select **W** (White)........................ W
   c) Select **R** (Red)........................ R
   d) Select **G** (Green)........................ G
   e) Select **B** (Blue)........................ B
   f) Select **Y** (Yellow)........................ Y
   g) Select **M** (Magenta)........................ M
   h) Select **C** (Cyan)........................ C
   i) Select **E** (Orange)........................ E
   j) Select **A** (Gray)........................ A
   k) Select **N** (Brown)........................ N
5. Press **F7** (return to document)........................ F7
6. Type text.
7. Press **Ctrl + F8** (Font menu)........................ Ctrl + F8
8. Select **C** (Print Color)........................ C
9. Select **K** (Black)........................ K
10. Press **F7** (return to document)........................ F7

continued...

Print Color (continued)

Creating a print color

1. Place cursor at beginning of text where new print color will be inserted.
2. Press **Ctrl + F8** (Font menu)........................ Ctrl + F8
3. Select **C** (Print Color).. C
4. Select **O** (Other).. O
5. Type in percentage of red.................................. **Option**
6. Enter.. ↵
7. Type in percentage of green.............................. **Option**
8. Enter.. ↵
9. Type in percentage of blue.................................**Option**
10. Enter.. ↵
11. Press **F7** (return to document)................................ F7
12. Type text.
13. Press **Ctrl + F8** (Font menu)........................ Ctrl + F8
14. Select **C** (Print Color).. C
15. Select **K** (Black).. K
16. Press **F7** (return to document)................................ F7

FORMS

WordPerfect uses forms to print in different sizes (length and width).

ADDING

1. Press **Shift + F7** (Print menu).................... Shift + F7
2. Select **S** (Select Printer).. S
3. Place cursor on desired printer that will contain the new form.
4. Select **E** (Edit).. E
5. Select **F** (Forms).. F
6. Select **A** (Add) .... A
7. Select one of the following options. **Option**
   - a) Select **S** (Standard).. S
   - b) Select **B** (Bond).. B
   - c) Select **H** (Letterhead)...................................... H
   - d) Select **L** (Labels).. L
   - e) Select **E** (Envelope)... E
   - f) Select **T** (Transparency).................................... T
   - g) Select **C** (Cardstock)... C
   - h) Select **A** [ALL OTHERS].................................. A

   NOTE: Selecting ***O*** *(Other) is for creating another form type that is unlisted.*
8. Select **S** (Form Size)... S

Forms (continued)

Adding (continued)

9. Select one of the following options: **Option**

   a) Select **S** (Standard - 8.5 X 11).. S

   b) Select **T** (Standard Wide - 11 X 8.5)........................ T

   c) Select **L** (Legal - 8.5 X 14).. L

   d) Select **G** (Legal Wide - 14 X 8.5)............................ G

   e) Select **E** (Envelope - 9.5 X 4)..................................... E

   f) Select **H** (Half Sheet - 5.5 X 8.5)............................. H

   g) Select **U** (US Government - 8 X 11)........................ U

   h) Select **A** (A4 - 210mm X 297mm)............................ A

   i) Select **W** (A4 - 297mm X 210mm)............................ W

   *NOTE: Selecting **O** (Other) is for creating another form size that is unlisted.*

10. Press **F7** (Exit).. F7
11. Press **F7** (Exit).. F7
12. Press **F7** .(Exit)... F7
13. Press **F7** (Exit).. F7
14. Press **F7** (return to document)..................................... F7

continued...

Forms (continued)

EDITING

1. Press **Shift + F7** (Print menu).................. Shift + F7
2. Select **S** (Select Printer).. S
3. Place cursor on printer that contains form.
4. Select **E** (Edit).. E
5. Select **F** (Forms).. F
6. Place cursor on form that will be edited.
7. Select **E** (Edit).. E
8. Enter one or more of the following options. **Option**
   a) Select **S** (Form Size).. S
   b) Select **O** (Orientation)....................................... O
   c) Select **I** (Initially Present)................................. I
   d) Select **L** (Location)... L
   e) Select **P** (Page Offsets - Top and Side)........... P
9. Press **F7** (Exit).. F7
10. Press **F7** (Exit).. F7
11. Press **F7** (Exit).. F7
12. Press **F7** (Exit).. F7
13. Press **F7** (return to document)................................ F7

continued...

Forms (continued)

DELETING

1. Press **Shift + F7** (Print menu).................... Shift + F7
2. Select **S** (Select Printer)... S
3. Place cursor on printer that contains form.
4. Select **E** (Edit).. E
5. Select **F** (Forms)... F
6. Place cursor on form that will be edited.
7. Select **D** (Delete)... D
8. Type **Y** .... Y
9. Press **F7** (Exit).. F7
10. Press **F7** (Exit).. F7
11. Press **F7** (Exit).. F7
12. Press **F7** (return to document)................................ F7

GRAPHICS

CREATING GRAPHIC

1. Press **Alt + F9** (Graphics)............................ Alt + F9
2. Select one of the following options Box Types menu: **Option**
   a) Select **F** (Figure)... F
   b) Select **T** (Table).. T
   c) Select **B** (Text Box).. B
   d) Select **U** (User-defined box)............................. U
3. Select **C** (Create).. C
4. Select **F** (Filename).. F
5. Type name of WordPerfect graphic file............... **Option**

   NOTE: If file is stored in a directory different from default then type in full path name.

   Example: c:\wp50\goodnews.wpg
6. Enter.. ↵
7. Press **F7** (return to document)................................ F7

continued..

CHANGING SIZE OF GRAPHIC

1. Press **Alt + F9** (Graphics).............................. Alt + F9
2. Select the appropriate box type: Option
   a) Select **F** (Figure).. F
   b) Select **T** (Table)... T
   c) Select **B** (Text Box).. B
   d) Select **U** (User-defined box)............................. U
3. Select **E** (Edit).. E
4. Type number of existing graphic.......................... Option
5. Enter.. ↵
6. Select **S** (Size).. S
7. Select **B** (Both Width and Height)............................ B
8. Type width.. Option
9. Enter.. ↵
10. Type height.. Option
11. Enter.. ↵
12. Press **F7** (return to document)................................ F7

continued...

ADDING CAPTION TO GRAPHIC

1. Press **Alt + F9** (Graphics)............................ Alt + F9
2. Select the appropriate box type: Option
   a) Select **F** (Figure).. F
   b) Select **T** (Table).. T
   c) Select **B** (Text Box)... B
   d) Select **U** (User-defined box)............................ U
3. Select **E** (Edit)... E
4. Type number of existing graphic......................... Option
5. Enter.. ↵
6. Select **C** (Caption).. C
7. Edit caption.
8. Press **F7** F7
9. Press **F7** (return to document)................................ F7

continued...

CHANGING TYPE OF GRAPHIC

1. Press **Alt + F9** (Graphics).............................. Alt + F9
2. Select the appropriate box type: Option
   a) Select **F** (Figure).. F
   b) Select **T** (Table).. T
   c) Select **B** (Text Box).. B
   d) Select **U** (User-defined box).............................. U
3. Select **E** (Edit).. E
4. Type number of existing graphic.......................... Option
5. Enter.. ↵
6. Select **T** (Type).. T
7. Select the appropriate type: Option
   a) Select **P** (Paragraph).. P
   b) Select **A** (Page).. A
   c) Select **C** (Character)... C
8. Press **F7** (return to document)................................ F7

continued...

MOVING GRAPHIC FIGURE

NOTE: If already in the Graphing submenu, steps 1-5 need not be repeated.

1. Press **Alt + F9** (Graphics).............................. Alt + F9
2. Select the appropriate box type: Option
   a) Select **F** (Figure).. F
   b) Select **T** (Table).. T
   c) Select **B** (Text Box).. B
   d) Select **U** (User-defined box)................................ U
3. Select **E** (Edit).. E
4. Type number of existing graphic........................ Option
5. Enter.. ↵
6. Select **E** (Edit).. E
7. Select **M** (Move).. M
8. Type horizontal position.. Option
9. Enter.. ↵
10. Type vertical position..Option
11. Enter.. ↵
12. Press **F7** F7
13. Press **F7** (return to document)................................ F7

continued...

SCALING GRAPHIC FIGURE

NOTE: *If already in the graphing submenu, steps 1-5 need not be repeated.*

1. Press **Alt + F9** (Graphics)........................ Alt + F9
2. Select the appropriate box type: Option
   a) Select **F** (Figure)........................ F
   b) Select **T** (Table)........................ T
   c) Select **B** (Text Box)........................ B
   d) Select **U** (User-defined box)........................ U
3. Select **E** (Edit)........................ E
4. Type number of existing graphic........................Option
5. Enter........................ ↵
6. Select **E** (Edit)........................ E
7. Select **S** (Scale)........................ S
8. Type X scale factor........................ Option
9. Enter........................ ↵
10. Type Y scale factor........................ Option
11. Enter........................ ↵
12. Press **F7** F7
13. Press **F7** (return to document)........................ F7

continued...

ROTATING GRAPHIC FIGURE

NOTE: If already in the graphing submenu, steps 1-5 need not be repeated.

1. Press **Alt + F9** (Graphics).............................. Alt + F9
2. Select the appropriate box type: Option
   a) Select **F** (Figure).............................. F
   b) Select **T** (Table).............................. T
   c) Select **B** (Text Box).............................. B
   d) Select **U** (User-defined box).............................. U
3. Select **E** (Edit).............................. E
4. Type number of existing graphic..............................Option
5. Enter.............................. ↵
6. Select **E** (Edit).............................. E
7. Select **R** (Rotate).............................. R
8. Type number of degrees for rotation.............................. Option
9. Enter.............................. ↵
10. Select mirrored image option:
    a) Enter (no).............................. ↵
    or OR
    b) Type **Y** (yes).............................. Y
11. Press **F7** F7
12. Press **F7** (return to document).............................. F7

continued...

NEW NUMBER

1. Place cursor at position in document for new number.
2. Press **Alt + F9** (Graphics).............................. Alt + F9
3. Select the appropriate box type: Option
    a) Select **F** (Figure)... F
    b) Select **T** (Table).. T
    c) Select **B** (Text Box).. B
    d) Select **U** (User-defined box)............................ U
4. Select **N** (New Number).. N
5. Type new graphic number....................................Option
6. Enter.. ↵

continued...

BORDER STYLE

1. Press **Alt + F3** (Reveal Codes).................... Alt + F3
2. Place cursor so it is immediately before graphic to be changed.
3. Press **Alt + F3** (Reveal Codes).................... Alt + F3
4. Press **Alt + F9** (Graphics).......................... Alt + F9
5. Select the appropriate box type: **Option**
   a) Select **F** (Figure).. F
   b) Select **T** (Table).. T
   c) Select **B** (Text Box)...................................... B
   d) Select **U** (User-defined box)............................ U
6. Select **O** (Options).. O
7. Select **B** (Border Style)....................................... B
8. Select the appropriate border style for the left side: **Option**
   a) Select **N** (None).. N
   b) Select **S** (Single)... S
   c) Select **D** (Double).. D
   d) Select **A** (Dashed).. A
   e) Select **O** (Dotted)... O
   f) Select **T** (Thick).. T
   g) Select **E** (Extra Thick)................................... E
9. Repeat Step 8 three times for the right, top and bottom sides.
10. Press **F7** (return to document).............................. F7

continued...

GRAY SHADING

1. Press **Alt + F3** (Reveal Codes).................... Alt + F3
2. Place cursor so it is immediately before graphic to be changed.
3. Press **Alt + F3** (Reveal Codes).................... Alt + F3
4. Press **Alt + F9** (Graphics)........................... Alt + F9
5. Select the appropriate box type: Option
   a) Select **F** (Figure).. F
   b) Select **T** (Table)... T
   c) Select **B** (Text Box)...................................... B
   d) Select **U** (User-defined box)........................ U
6. Select **O** (Options)... O
7. Select **G** (Gray Shading - % of black).................... G
8. Type percentage... Option
9. Enter... ↵
10. Press **F7** (return to document)............................ F7

continued...

PRINTING GRAPHICS

1. Place cursor on the page that contains graphic(s).
2. Press **Shift + F7** (Print menu).................. Shift + F7
3. Select **P** (Page).. P

HORIZONTAL LINE

1. Press **Alt + F9** (Graphics)........................... Alt + F9
2. Select **L** (Line).. L
3. Select **H** (Horizontal Line)................................ H
4. Press **F7** (return to document)........................ F7

CUSTOMIZED HORIZONTAL LINE

1. Press **Alt + F9** (Graphics)........................... Alt + F9
2. Select **L** (Line).. L
3. Select **H** (Horizontal Line)................................ H
4. Enter one or more of the following options: **Option**
   a) Select **H** (Horizontal Position)...................... H
   b) Select **L** (Length of Line).............................. L
   c) Select **W** (Width of Line)............................... W
   d) Select **G** (Gray Shading - % of black)............... G
5. Press **F7** (return to document)........................ F7

continued...

VERTICAL LINE

1. Press **Alt + F9** (Graphics)............................ Alt + F9
2. Select **L** (Line).. L
3. Select **V** (Vertical Line).. V
4. Press **F7** (return to document).............................. F7

CUSTOMIZED VERTICAL LINE

1. Press **Alt + F9** (Graphics).......................... Alt + F9
2. Select **L** (Line).. L
3. Select **V** (Vertical Line).. V
4. Enter one or more of the following options: **Option**
   a) Select **H** (Horizontal Position).......................... H
   b) Select **V** (Vertical Position)............................. V
   c) Select **L** (Length of Line)................................. L
   d) Select **W** (Width of Line)................................. W
   e) Select **G** (Gray Shading - % of black)............. G
5. Press **F7** (return to document).............................. F7

STYLES

Styles retain format codes and/or text for repeated use in a document.

CREATING

1. Press **Alt + F8** (Style)........ Alt + F8
2. Select **C** (Create)........ C
3. Select **N** (Name)........ N
4. Type name of style........ **Option**
5. Enter........ ↵
6. Select **D** (Description)........ D
7. Type in description of style.
8. Enter........ ↵
9. Select **T** (Type)........ T
10. Select the type of style:
    a) Select **P** (Paired)........ P
    or .... OR
    b) Select **O** (Open)........ O
11. Select **C** (Codes)........ C
12. Insert codes and/or text.
13. Press **F7** (Exit)........ F7
14. Press **F7** (Exit)........ F7
15. Press **F7** (return to document)........ F7

continued...

USING PAIRED STYLE FOR NEW TEXT

1. Place cursor at position where style will be inserted.
2. Press **Alt + F8** (Style).. Alt + F8
3. Place cursor on style to be selected.
4. Select **O** (On).. O
5. Type text.
6. Press Right Arrow (turn style off)................................ →

USING PAIRED STYLE FOR EXISTING TEXT

1. Place cursor at beginning of text for paired style.
2. Press **Alt + F4** (Block).. Alt + F4
3. Highlight text. (See Block Text section.)
4. Press **Alt + F8** (Style).. Alt + F8
5. Place cursor on style to be selected.
6. Select **O** (On).. O

USING OPEN STYLE

1. Place cursor at position where style will be inserted.
2. Press **Alt + F8** (Style).. Alt + F8
3. Place cursor on style to be selected.
4. Select **O** (On).. O

continued...

Styles (continued)

EDITING A STYLE

1. Press **Alt + F8** (Style).................................. Alt + F8
2. Place cursor on style to be selected.
3. Select **E** (Edit).. E
4. Edit text and codes.
5. Press **F7** (Exit).. F7
6. Press **F7** (Exit).. F7
7. Press **F7** (return to document).............................. F7

DELETING A STYLE

1. Press **Alt + F8** (Style).................................. Alt + F8
2. Place cursor on style to be deleted.
3. Select **D** (Delete).. D
4. Type **Y** (yes)... Y
5. Press **F7** (return to document).............................. F7

continued...

SAVING/UPDATING STYLES DOCUMENT

A styles document contains a list of style(s) that can be applied to other documents.

1. Press **Alt + F8** (Style).................................. Alt + F8
2. Select **S** (Save).. S
3. Type in name of style document with "sty" extension.. Option

   Example: Letter.sty

4. Enter.. ↵

   NOTE: Type "Y" to update style document if it already exists.

5. Press **F7** (return to document)................................ F7

RETRIEVING STYLES DOCUMENT

1. Press **Alt + F8** (Style).................................. Alt + F8
2. Select **R** (Retrieve).. R
3. Type in name of style document...........................Option
4. Enter.. ↵

PASSWORD

Adding a password to a document prevents it from being retrieved or edited without entering the password.

ADD/CHANGE

1. Retrieve document that will have password added to it.
2. Press **Ctrl + F5** (Text In/Out menu)............ Ctrl + F5
3. Select **P** (Password).. P
4. Select **A** (Add/Change)...................................... A
5. Type in password.

   NOTE: A password can contain up to 24 characters.

6. Enter.. ↵
7. Type in password again.
8. Enter.. ↵

   NOTE: It is impossible to retrieve the document if the password is forgotten.

REMOVE

1. Retrieve document that will have password removed.
2. Press **Ctrl + F5** (Text In/Out menu)............ Ctrl + F5
3. Select **P** (Password).. P
4. Select **R** (Remove).. R

continued...

ADVANCE

Advance tells printer to advance to a specific position in document.

1. Place cursor at position where advance will be.
2. Press **Shift + F8** (Format menu).............. Shift + F8
3. Select **O** (Other).. O
4. Select **A** (Advance).. A
5. Select one of the following from the advance menu: Option
   a) Select **U** (Up).. U
   b) Select **D** (Down).. D
   c) Select **I** (Line).. I
   d) Select **L** (Left).. L
   e) Select **R** (Right)... R
   f) Select **P** (Position)....................................... P
6. Type in number for advance.................................. Option
7. Enter.. ↵
8. Press **F7** (return to document)................................ F7

LINE NUMBERING

1. Retrieve document for line numbering.
2. Press **Shift + F8** (Format menu).............. Shift + F8
3. Select **L** (Line Format).. L
4. Select **N** (Line Numbering)...................................... N
5. Type **Y** (yes).. Y
6. Press **F7** (return to document)................................ F7

CHANGING SPACE BETWEEN CHARACTERS

NOTE: This feature must be supported by printer to work successfully.

1. Place cursor before character(s) to have spacing change.
2. Press **Shift + F8** (Format menu)............... Shift + F8
3. Select **O** (Other)............... O
4. Select **P** (Printer Functions)............... P
5. Select **W** (Word Spacing)............... W
6. Enter............... ↵
7. Select **P** (Percent of Optimal)............... P
8. Type number............... Option
9. Enter............... ↵
10. Press **F7** (return to document)............... F7

LINE HEIGHT

1. Place cursor before line to have line height change.
2. Press **Shift + F8** (Format menu)............... Shift + F8
3. Select **L** (Line)............... L
4. Select **H** (Height)............... H
5. Select **F** (Fixed)............... F
6. Type height............... Option
7. Enter............... ↵

   NOTE: To make the height automatic, Select A instead of steps 5-7.

8. Press **F7** (return to document)............... F7

PRINTER COMMAND

Printer Commands sends codes directly to printer. See printer manual for reference.

1. Place cursor at position for printer command.
2. Press **Shift + F8** (Format menu).............. Shift + F8
3. Select **O** (Other).. O
4. Select **P** (Printer Functions)................................... P
5. Select **P** (Printer Command).................................. P
6. Select **C** (Command)... C
7. Type command.
8. Enter.. ↵
9. Press **F7** (return to document)................................ F7

SETUP

1. Press **Shift + F1**.. Shift + F1
2. Make setup changes.
3. Press **F7** (return to document)................................ F7

HELP

1. Press **F3** (Help).. F3
2. Look up feature.
3. Enter (to return to document)...................................... ↵

EXIT/QUIT

Note: Verify screen is cleared or document has been updated.

1. Press **F7**.. F7
2. Select **N**.. N
3. Select **Y**.. Y

SHELL (DOS access)

1. Press **Ctrl + F1**.. Ctrl + F1
2. Select **G**.. G
3. Enter DOS commands.
4. Type **e**.. e
5. Type **x**.. x
6. Type **i**.. i
7. Type **t**.. t
8. Enter.. ↵

SAVE

DOS TEXT FILE

1. Retrieve document.
2. Press **Ctrl + F5** (Text In/Out menu)................ Ctrl + F5
3. Select **T** (Dos Text) .... T
4. Select **S** (Save).. S
5. Type the name of the DOS text file........................**Option**
6. Enter.. ↵

WORDPERFECT 4.2 FILE

1. Retrieve document.
2. Press **Ctrl + F5** (Text In/Out menu)............... Ctrl + F5
3. Select **W** (Save WP 4.2).. W
4. Type the name of WordPerfect 4.2 document........**Option**
5. Enter.. ↵

INDEX

Advance Printer 152
Append 42
Automatic Reference 123-124
Base Font
  Change 125
  Change Appearance
    Before Typing Text 127
    Existing Text 128
  Change Font Size
    Before Typing Text 125
    Existing Text 126
Block Protect 47
Block Text (Highlighting) 9
Boilerplate Text 21
Bolding Text 37
Bottom Margin 22
Calculation Column 61
Calculations 58-61
Cancelling a Print Request 18
Capitalization 50
Case Conversion 50
Centering
  Before Typing Text 31
  Block of Text 31
  Existing Text 31
  Heading Over Column 32
  Page Top to Bottom 32
Change Appearance
  Before Typing Text 127
Change Appearance of Existing text 128
Change Base Font 125
Change Print Color 129
Change Size of Base Font 125
Change Size of Base
  Font of Existing Text 126
Change Space Between Characters 153
Check Menu 81
Clear Screen 7
Codes Delete 13
Columns
  Center Heading 32
  Create 51
  Display 52
  Editing 52
  Math 57
  Newspaper 51
  Off 52
  Parallel 51
Combining Documents 21
Concordance (Index) 121-122
Conditional End of Page 46
Copy Text
  Block of Text 38
  External Copy 41
  Sentence/Paragraph/Page 39
  Rectangular Block of Text 40
  Tabular Column 40
Create
  Columns 51
  Document 3
  Document Comments 93
  Document Summary 14
  Document Assembly (Boilerplate) 21
  Footnotes/Endnotes 55
  Headers/Footers 53
  Graphics 135
  Index (Concordance) 121-122
  Macros 101
  Merged Document 66
  Outline 87-89
  Primary File 64
  Print Color 130
  Secondary File (Data file) 62-63
  Styles 147
Cursor
  Highlighting 9
  Movements Within a Column 52
  Movements Within a Document 4
  Movements Using The Go To Key 5
Date
  Code 91
  Text 91
Decimal Align Tabs (Tab Style) 25
Deleting
  Block Highlight 12
  Character 11
  Codes 13
  Document (From List Files) 92
  End of Line 12
  End of Page 12
  Forms 134
  Parts of Word 11
  Previous Character 11
  Several Lines 12
  Styles 149
  Undelete 13
  Word 11
Delete Document (From List Files) 92
Document Assembly
  Boilerplate Text 21
  Combining Documents 21
Document Comments
  Create 93
  Display 94
  Edit 94

continued...

Document Summary 14
DOS Access (Shell) 155
Dot Leader Tab (Tab Style) 25
Double Word Menu 82
Edit
  Column 52
  Delete 11-13
  Footnotes/Endnotes 56
  Forms 133
  Headers/Footers 54
  Insert 10
  Macro 104
  Style 149
  Text 10-13
  Typeover 10
  Undelete 13
Eliminate Blank Lines 65
Endnotes
  Create 55
  Delete 56
  Edit 56
Envelopes (Merge) 67-69
Escape 105-106
  Change Repetition Number 106
  Repeat Character 106
Exit/Quit 154
Extended Search 78
External Copy 41
Flush Right 36
Fonts
  Change Appearance Before
    Typing Text 127
  Change Appearance of Existing text 128
  Change Base Font 125
  Change Print Color 129
  Change Size of Base Font Before
    Typing Text 125
  Change Size of Base Font
    of Existing Text 126
  Create Print Color 130
Footers
  Create 53
  Edit 54
Footnotes
  Create 55
  Delete 56
  Edit 56
Formatting a Disk 1
Forms
  Adding 131-132
  Deleting 134
  Editing 133
Formulas 57
Forward Search 77
Function Key Illustration c
Global Select 115
Go To key 5
Graphics
  Add Caption 137
  Border Style 143
  Change Size 136
  Change Type 138
  Create 135
  Customize Horizontal Line 145
  Customize Vertical Line 146
  Gray Shading 144
  Horizontal Line 145
  Move Figure 139
  New Number 142
  Printing 145
  Rotating Figure 141
  Scaling Figure 140
  Vertical line 146
Hanging Indent 29
Hard Page Break
  Delete 46
  Insert 46
Hard Space 48
Headers
  Create 53
  Edit 54
Help 154
Highlighting (Block On) 9
Hyphenation
  On 48
  Off 49
  H-Zone 49
H-Zone
Indent
  Every Line 28
  First Line 28
  Left/Right 29
  Hanging 29
Index (Concordance) 121-122
Insert 10
Justification On/Off 35
Labels 70-76
Line
  Draw 107
  Height 153
  Numbering 152
  Spacing 30
List Files 92
Loading Procedure 2
Macros
  Create/Replace 101
  Edit 104
  Pause 102

continued...

- Playback ... 103
- Stopping ... 103
- Margin Release ... 23
- Margins
  - Left and Right ... 22
  - Top and Bottom ... 22
  - Release ... 23
- Math
  - Calculation Column ... 61
  - Calculations ... 58-61
  - Defining Columns ... 57
  - Formulas ... 57
  - Grand Total ... 60
  - Math Off ... 61
  - Subtotal ... 59
  - Total ... 59
- Merge
  - Create Merged Document ... 66
  - Create Primary File ... 64
  - Create Secondary File ... 62-63
  - Eliminate Blank Lines ... 65
  - Envelopes ... 67-69
  - Move and Copy Text ... 38-41
  - Multiple Width Labels ... 72-76
  - Save Merged Document ... 66
  - Sentence/Paragraph/Page ... 39
  - Single Width Labels ... 70-71
  - Sort (Secondary File) ... 111-112
- Merge Sort ... 111-112
- Move and Copy Text
  - Block Of Text ... 38
  - Rectangular Block Of Text ... 40
  - Sentence/Paragraph/Page ... 39
  - Tabular Column ... 40
- Multiple Line Sort ... 110-111
  - (See Also Sort and Select)
- Multiple Width Labels ... 72-76
- Newspaper Columns ... 51
- New Page Number ... 45
- Not Found Menu ... 81-82
- Orphan
  - (See Widow/Orphan Protection On/Off)
- Outline
  - Change Outline Numbering Styles ... 90
  - Create ... 87-89
  - Remove Outline Numbers ... 89
- Page
  - Block Protect ... 47
  - Center Top to Bottom ... 32
  - Conditional End of Page ... 46
  - Hard Page Break ... 46
  - New Page Number (Repagination) ... 45
  - Numbering ... 44
  - Size/Type ... 43
  - Widow/Orphan Protect On/Off ... 47
- Page Numbering ... 44
- Paper Size/Type ... 43
- Parallel Columns ... 51
- Password
  - Add/Change ... 151
  - Remove ... 151
- Playback Macro ... 103
- Primary File ... 64-65
- Print Color ... 128
  - Change Color ... 129
  - Create Color ... 130
- Printer Command ... 154
- Printing
  - Block ... 17
  - Document ... 15
  - Document on Screen ... 15
  - Cancel Print Job Before it Begins ... 18
  - Cancelling a Request ... 18
  - Change Color ... 129
  - Create Print Color ... 130
  - From List Files ... 17
  - Graphics ... 145
  - Stored Document ... 15
  - View Document on Screen ... 16
  - View List of Print Jobs ... 19
- Quit ... 154
- Redline Text ... 95
  - Block of Text ... 95
  - Remove ... 96
- Rename Document From List Files ... 92
- Repagination (New Page Number) ... 45
- Repetition ... 106
- Replace ... 79
- Retrieve
  - Document ... 8
  - From List Files ... 8
  - Styles ... 150
- Reveal Codes
  - (See Delete Codes)
- Reverse Search ... 78
- Save
  - Boilerplate Text ... 21
  - Document ... 6-7
  - DOS Text File ... 155
  - Macro ... 101-102
  - Styles ... 150
  - WordPerfect 4.2 File ... 155
- Search
  - Forward ... 77
  - Reverse ... 78
  - Extended ... 78
- Secondary File ... 62-63
- Select Only ... 113-114
- Setup ... 154

continued...

Shell (DOS Access) 155
Single Width Labels 70-71
Sort
  Global Select 115
  Merge Sort 111-112
  Multiple Line Sort 110-111
  Select Only 113-114
  Single Line Sort 108-110
  Sort & Select Secondary
    Merge File 118-119
  Sort & Select (Single &
    Multiple Line Sort) 116-117
  Sort & Select
    Secondary Merge File 118-119
    Single & Multiple Line Sort 116-117
Spacing
  Between Characters 153
  Line 30
Speller
  Check Menu 81
  Double Word Menu 82
  Not Found Menu 81-82
  Speller Utility 83-84
Speller Utility 83-84
Split Screen (Windows) 98
  Close Window 98
  Save and Exit Document Two 99
  Switch Documents 100
Startup Procedure 2
Strikeout Text 96
  Remove 96
Styles
  Create 147
  Delete 149
  Editing 149
  Open Style 148
  Paired Style For Existing Text 148
  Paired Style For New Text 148
  Retrieve Styles Document 150
  Saving/Updating Styles Document 150
Super/Subscript
  Character 80
  Block of Text 80
Switch Documents 100
Tab
  Align 27
  Left-Justified 24
  Multiple 26
  Ruler 97
  Set 24-26
  Styles 25
Tab Align 27
Tab Ruler 97
Tab Styles 25
Table of Contents 120
Tabular Column 40
Thesaurus 85-86
Top Margin 22
Type Through
  Character 20
  Line 20
Typeover 10
Undelete 13
Underlining
  Before Text 33
  Existing Text 33
  Double Underline Existing Text 34
  Double Underline New Text 34
  Underline Spaces and Tabs 34
Underlining Style 34
View Document On Screen 16
View List of Print Jobs 19
Widow/Orphan Protect On/Off 47
Windows (Split Screen) 98-99